YOUR UNIQUE SELF

AN INTEGRAL PATH TO SUCCESS 3.0

MARC GAFNI

KATE MALONEY

Foreword & Afterword by Ken Wilber
Foreword by Barbara Marx Hubbard
Special Dialogue with John Mackey

Edited by Jules Cazedessus

Excerpts from Your Unique Self: The Radical Path to Personal Enlightenment

Praise For Marc Gafni's Work on
YOUR UNIQUE SELF

"Marc is a deeply inspiring and talented transformational teacher."
— Deepak Chopra, author of *Spiritual Solutions:
Answers to Life's Greatest Challenges*

"Dr. Marc Gafni has written a brilliant book, *Your Unique Self*, which I believe is essential reading. *Your Unique Self* articulates a bold evolutionary, spiritual, philosophy that calls every individual to realize their Unique Self and give their Unique Gifts in an evolutionary context. Gafni, together with his colleague Ken Wilber, is a bold visionary and a catalytic voice for the newly emergent World Spirituality movement, which combines the best of premodern, modern, and postmodern insight. I highly recommend this book."
— John Mackey, CEO of Whole Foods
and Chair of Center for Integral Wisdom

"Dr. Marc Gafni's Integral Unique Self teaching is seminal. What you hold in your hands is a radically exciting and ground-breaking book that will change forever not only how you think about enlightenment, but how you understand from a post mental physical perspective, the very nature of human life itself. The Unique Self work is magnificent, and it belongs among the 'great books.' It offers what may arguably be one of the most significant contemporary evolutions of enlightenment teaching. Unique Self brings together East and West in a higher integral embrace of stunning implications. Unique Self is a pivotal step toward an authentic enlightenment."
— Ken Wilber, author of *A Brief History of Everything*

"With exceptional brilliance and an awakened heart, Dr. Marc Gafni speaks to all of us who are interested in the evolution of consciousness. His teachings on the Unique Self enlightenment are essential for the next stage in our evolution. They have emerged from his direct experience and I highly recommend them."
— Michael Bernard Beckwith, author of *Spiritual Liberation:
Fulfilling Your Soul's Potential*

"*Your Unique Self* is a great read. As is obvious from even flipping through its pages, Dr. Marc Gafni not only understands the material, but also has lived it. The book is both thorough and fun, and will provoke deep thoughts. I meant to scan it on vacation and ended up reading it cover to cover in one sitting. It's a book that is worth many readings. It will both fascinate you in its insights and annoy you that you haven't read this book until now."
— Dave Logan, PhD, New York Times #1 bestselling co-author
of *Tribal Leadership*; former Associate Dean, USC Marshall
School of Business

"Dr. Marc Gafni's teaching on the Unique Self radically evolves the way we understanding and realize enlightenment. He is a great teacher of both heart and mind. His penetrating depth, practicality, and heartfelt charisma will change your life."
— John Gray, author of *Men Are from Mars, Women Are from Venus*

"This is a coherent, comprehensive and amazing book from an amazing mind on a challenging topic. Using the concept of the "Unique Self" as the essential reality behind all forms of the self, the author succeeds in integrating not only the historical East-West polarities regarding the nature of the self, the variables of spiritual practice and the meaning of enlightenment, but also the antinomies between psychotherapy and the spiritual traditions. His redefinition, extension and integration of the core meanings of healing, wholeness and the self will expand the consciousness of all readers. I compliment the author's intellectual and spiritual achievement and recommend it to all travelers on the journey to enlightenment."
— Harville Hendrix, PhD, author of *Getting the Love You Want:
A Guide for Couples*

"If you've bumped up against the paradox of experiencing your life daily as a unique individual, yet continually hearing from spiritual circles that 'we're all one' (and knowing that there's something to that idea too), then read Marc Gafni's awesome book *Your Unique Self*. Marc resolves the paradox beautifully, and in the process helps connect each of us to our unique gifts and opportunities in the world."
— Eben Pagan, Internet Marketing Guru

"No one book has inspired me to cherish myself, respect others and have hope for both this country and this world more fully than *Your Unique Self*. With insights as sharp as a knife and words that hone its blade, Rabbi Gafni holds before us the mirror of our unique selves and the molecular, spiritual, internal and external paths we might explore to enhance that uniqueness. An extraordinary future classic. *Your Unique Self* gives my Unique Self shivers."

— Warren Farrell, PhD, author of *Why Men Are the Way They Are* and *The Myth of Male Power*

"Marc Gafni's brilliant intellect and spiritual passion make him a force to be reckoned with. His deep knowledge and advocacy of Abrahamic mysticism, coupled with his inspired vision of a World Spirituality, offer a unique and significant contribution to the evolution of our understanding of God, religion and Spirit in the 21st century."

— Andrew Cohen, founder of EnlightenNext, author of *Evolutionary Enlightenment*

"Marc Gafni's overflowing heart and transmission of the Unique Self teaching profoundly moves me. Dr. Marc holds the lineage energy of the great Hasidic masters of Kabbalah, which he brings with him into the visionary initiative of Center for Integral Wisdom. There is little doubt in my mind that *Your Unique Self* will become one of the classic texts that forms the World Spirit vision that our world needs so deeply. This is a book and a teacher that we all very much need."

— Lama Surya Das, author of *Awakening the Buddha Within: Tibetan Wisdom for the Western World* and founder of the Dzogchen Meditation Centers

"Marc Gafni's *Your Unique Self* is the great invitation to live a meaningful life that we have all been waiting for. This book is especially for anyone who has ever wondered if they have a unique calling or purpose in life. The answer is YES and you are well on your way to learn how to live a life of infinite creativity, passion and possibility. The next step of the journey is to read this brilliant guide to discover WHO YOU ARE and WHAT YOU ARE here to uniquely experience, express and expand on behalf of the whole."

— Paul Taylor, CEO, Global Citizen Consulting; former Global VP, The Coca-Cola Company

"Marc Gafni is a brilliant teacher and heart master with a rare capacity for empathy and a gift for creating community. This book contains the essence of his teaching on what it means to live from an enlightened life from a ground of one's own personal uniqueness. A truly ground-shifting book, it offers a perspective on personal transformation that integrates insights of traditional and postmodern wisdom. Reading it can change your understanding not only of your own path, but also of what it means to live a life of inner contemplation and transformative service in the world. This is a book that deserves to become a classic."
— Sally Kempton, author of *Meditation for the Love of It*

"Dr. Marc Gafni's writing eloquently demonstrates the essentially mental—and futile—conclusion that there ever could be separation between 'I' (oneself, me) and 'Presence' (no-I, unity). Both 'I' and 'unity' are radiant refractions of the infinite mystery of beingness conscious of itself. I salute and support his expression and recognition of the uniqueness of each in all."
— Gangaji, author of *Hidden Treasure: Uncovering the Truth in Your Life*

"Dr. Marc Gafni's teaching on Unique Self is simply awesome."
— Diane Musho Hamilton, Zen teacher and master facilitator

"One of the great problems with so much of modern 'new age spirituality' is that it lacks depth. Dr. Gafni, in his new book *Your Unique Self*, has written an emotionally moving and intellectually stimulating book that moves the reader to ponder deeply many of the very core elements of their faith and practice. His discussion of enlightenment within a modern context is worth the price of the book alone! I heartily recommend this book to all serious pilgrims on the religious or spiritual road."
— Rabbi Avram Davis, Ph.D. author of *The Way Of Flame*
Founder, Chochmat Halev Educational Center

"Grounded as it is in decades of research and first-person spiritual and psychological exploration, Gafni's book makes an enormous contribution to contemporary understanding of what is possible for human beings."
— Prof. Michael E. Zimmerman, Former Director of the Center for Humanities and the Arts at CU Boulder, author of *Eclipse of the Self: The Development of Heidegger's Concept of Authenticity*

"Dr. Marc Gafni is simply one of the great brilliant overflowing heart minds of the generation. I heard his teaching on Unique Self at the first Integral Spiritual Experience and it blew my mind and melted my heart. This book is a must read. For anyone who wants to fulfill their purpose on this earth, Marc is one of the great new voices in the Translucent Revolution."
— Arjuna Ardagh, author of *Awakening into Oneness*
and *Leap Before You Look*

"Marc Gafni's wisdom and insight moved my heart and inspired my mind. This new teacher of spirit... is sure to become an important voice in helping to chart our soul paths in the new millennium."
— Barbara De Angelis, PhD, author of *Real Moments*

"*Your Unique Self* is picking up on this new emerging sense of self which emerges at the second tier of consciousness. It's very powerful, this teaching of Unique Self, because it has to escape a very heavy communal pressures of the 'we' who suggests that after spiritual practice you realize that there is no essential individuality at all. Well, that's not true. Thank God for this Unique Self teaching; that's where creativity is. In your genius you've hit upon what the very unique properties are of this seventh station understanding of self."
— Don Beck, developmental theorist, co-author of *Spiral Dynamics*

"Marc's Gafni's spiritual democracy is the evolutionary unfolding of love and intelligence in our era. This book is dangerous because it contains ideas which, if put into practice, could bridge the long-time dichotomy between Western and Eastern spirituality and provide a revolutionary method to transcend your ego-binding separateness while still retaining your specialness. *Your Unique Self* is dangerous for a second reason as well: Not only is this volume way brilliant, it breaks through your head and opens your heart. In the age of the ruling elites—be they spiritual or political is over—the future of our world depends on your enlightenment. For all of our sake, please read on..."
— Sharon Gannon, founder of the Jivamukti Yoga Method

"In response to a culture wandering and aimless, Dr. Gafni has produced nothing less than a context of meaning that can draw us into the heart of Spirit's next creative move."
— Sam Alexander, Presbyterian Minister

"I predict that history will note *Your Unique Self* as being a seminal work in helping to accelerate the evolution of the consciousness of the planet in the 21st century. In a truly momentous book of integrated philosophy by Marc Gafni, the Tantric view that we are in essence unique reflections of the Supreme Self is presented in an unprecedented way. For the masses to make an inspired personal choice to glorify the Universal as singularly diverse individuals will be the legacy of this great book."
— John Friend, founder of Anusara Yoga

"It is very rare that one comes across a teacher or a book that is 'changing the game.' My friend, Dr. Marc Gafni, is such a teacher. He is a rare combination of brilliance, depth, and heart. Marc's teaching on the Unique Self in an evolutionary context is 'changing the game.'"
— Michael Murphy, founder of Esalen Institute,
    author of *Golf in the Kingdom*

"*Your Unique Self* is one of the most brilliant, provocative, and original books of the new century. Dr. Marc Gafni has fused together the deepest insights of the Eastern and Western mystery traditions to provide an evolutionary road map for the Great Birth that is arising in and through our contemporary world crisis. This is indispensable reading. The vision of the Unique Self is absolutely essential for the next step of evolution and I cannot recommend it highly enough."
— Andrew Harvey, author of *The Hope: A Guide to Sacred Activism*

"Marc, a fellow drinker at the holy taverns has written a fine, fine book. Kabbalists say a Day of Tikkun (evolution, soul-repair) is coming. There are great stories here from the Hasidic masters and from Marc's own life, honoring the unique soulmaking that has brought you to this moment. This beautiful book will deepen that astonishing mystery and awaken you to the individual beauty of your path."
— Coleman Barks, author of *Rumi: The Big Red Book*

"Marc Gafni is an important and exciting new spiritual guide. With humility, genuine warmth, and enormous power, Gafni merges ancient wisdom with his profound insights to lead us back to ourselves."
— Richard Carlson, author of *Don't Sweat the Small Stuff*

YOUR UNIQUE SELF
AN INTEGRAL PATH TO SUCCESS 3.0

MARC GAFNI
President, Center for Integral Wisdom

KATE MALONEY
Co-Chairperson of the Board, Center for Integral Wisdom

Foreword & Afterword by Ken Wilber
Co-Founder, Center for Integral Wisdom

Foreword Barbara Marx Hubbard
Founder, Foundation for Conscious Evolution
Wisdom Council, Center for Integral Wisdom

Special Dialogue with John Mackey
Chairperson of the Board, Center for Integral Wisdom

Edited by Jules Cazedessus

Integral Publishers
1418 N, Jefferson Ave.
Tucson, Arizona 85712

ISBN: 978-0-9904419-3-9

Cover by QT Punque

There are two great questions that every person must answer:

Who are you?

Are you willing to play a larger game?

The answer to the second question depends on the answer to the first question.

You are an irreducibly unique expression of All-That-Is, that lives in you, as you, and through you.

Your Unique Self emerges from your unique perspective. Your unique perspective births your unique gifts. Your unique gifts have the ability address a unique need in your unique circle of intimacy and influence— a need that can be uniquely addressed only by you.

Giving your unique gift, addressing the unique need that can be addressed by you and you alone, is your unique obligation, your unique responsibility and your unique joy. It is how you become the hero of your life.

Living your Unique Self, giving your unique gift and addressing your unique needs is what it means to wake up, grow and show up.

Showing up is the largest game you can play.

CONTENTS

WAKE UP, GROW UP, SHOW UP: SUCCESS 3.0

TO ENSURE A SUCCESSFUL FUTURE for our species and our planet, the evolution of consciousness is the most critical imperative of our time.

The evolution of consciousness is in reality, nothing less than enlightenment itself. What is enlightenment? Let's start with what it's not: Enlightenment is not spiritual perfection. It is not a constant state of meditative bliss which is indifferent to the world. Enlightenment is no longer just for exceptional individuals who join ashrams or spend decades meditating on mountaintops. The old paradigm of top-down leadership, the *sage on the stage*, and command and control, expressed itself in the spiritual world with the assumption that enlightenment was reserved only for an elite few. It is time to democratize enlightenment—to bring this sacred human imperative down from the mountains to the masses.

What enlightenment does mean in a post-postmodern context is the realization that we are—at our core—inseparable from All-That-Is. Enlightenment means we are holding a worldcentric and even cosmocentric consciousness from which we experience both compassion for and identity with the larger world. This is how we free up the enlightened creativity of the entrepreneurial spirit. It is only such an enlightened entrepreneurial creativity that will infuse our lives with aliveness, purpose and potency. It is only such aliveness, potency and purpose that will unleash the level of innovation necessary to survive and thrive at this pivotal juncture in history.

This is why enlightenment is, in fact, fundamental to our new narrative of success. It is the body/mind/heart technology that is absolutely essential if we are to transcend the contractions of individual and national ego that are the source of so much suffering. Only an enlightened community of nations can take this planet to the next critical step.

Success can no longer be limited to the individual level. It's no longer merely a question of "How can I be I successful?" but rather "How can We be successful?" There is no longer an awake individual who stands alone or separate from the larger context of family, community, tribe or country. Success is only possible in the largest evolutionary context—inclusive of the entire global enterprise of human consciousness and culture. A new vision of success must address the challenges of our time in a way that every one of us can survive, thrive and prosper.

The purpose of Success 3.0 is two-fold. First, to make explicit the limiting vision of success that currently drives our lives and dreams both as individuals and as a larger global community. Second, to articulate a more compelling, courageous and comprehensive vision of success. This new vision of success reflects the deepest knowledge we have today—drawing from all the different strands of Integral wisdom, premodern, modern and postmodern. In our 3.0 schema, as articulated by John Mackey, zero is premodern or traditional wisdom, 1.0 is modern wisdom, and 2.0 is postmodern wisdom. Our goal is to map a new Integral vision—Success 3.0.

At the core of this new vision of success is to live your Unique Self. Your Unique Self is reality *Godding* through you. Your Unique Self is the song only you can sing, the poem only you can write. Your Unique Self is your irreducibly unique way of loving, laughing, being and becoming that is yours and yours alone. The realization of your Unique Self informs you that the singular constellation of sacred evolutionary synchronicities that formed you have never and will never, ever occur again.

To successfully live your Unique Self you need to *Wake Up, Grow Up and Show Up*. Success 3.0 offers a new operating system to do just this. It is the critical calling of our time.

Wake Up

To wake up means to move beyond the narcissistic self-involvement with your own contracted story. Most people live lives limited by their contracted self, consumed by the petty details of their story. But when you wake up, you awaken to the deeper truth: You are not merely a skin-encapsulated ego—your True Self is an inextricable, indivisible part of the love-intelligence, of the All-That-Is flowing through you. So to wake up is to wake up to the true nature of reality, to blow your mind as a separate, alienated self, and to know your True Self, which presages a new and revolutionary Unique Self enlightenment.

Grow Up

To grow up means to up-level your consciousness. Your level of consciousness is the set of implicit organizing principles forming your worldview. These ascending levels or structures of consciousness have been mapped by extensive cross-cultural research by leading ego-developmental scientists over the past fifty years. For example, it has been shown that human beings in healthy development evolve from egocentric to ethnocentric to worldcentric to cosmocentric consciousness. Each level expands your felt sense of love and empathy to wider and wider circles of caring.

At first, your caring and concern is limited to you and your immediate circle. At the second level—ethnocentric—your identity expands to a felt-sense of empathy and connections with your larger communal context. At the third level—worldcentric—your identity shifts to a felt empathy with all living humanity. At the fourth level — cosmocentric —you move beyond mere humanity and experience a felt-sense of responsibility and empathy for all sentient beings throughout all of time, backwards and forwards.

This last move has also been described in Clare Graves' developmental theory as the evolution from first-tier to second-tier consciousness. One of the key findings of developmental research is that as you up-level to ever-higher stages of second-tier consciousness, your unique perspective becomes readily available. Said simply, according to leading developmental theorists, the more you grow up, the more your Unique Self comes online. Indeed, having ready access to your unique perspective and your unique quality of intimacy is the way to unfold the highest levels of consciousness.

Show Up

To be successful means to live the unique life that is yours to live and give the unique gifts that are yours to give. Your success, therefore, looks different then any one else's success (so you might as well be successful in your own life because you cannot be successful in anyone else's).

To live your unique life and give your unique gifts is what it means to be the hero of your life. This practice is called, in the terminology of Success 3.0, showing up. To show up as your Unique Self and give your unique gifts and live your unique taste is to awaken as evolution—as the personal face of the evolutionary process.

World Spirituality is based on the realization that every human being is both part of the whole and at the same time a high priest or priestess in their religion of one. The core obligation, joy, and responsibility of each Unique Self is to answer the call and give its unique gift, which fills a unique need in the cosmos.

Success 3.0

To be successful means to wake up to who you really are.

To be successful means to grow up to higher and higher levels of consciousness. When you grow up to your highest level of consciousness, you emerge as a fully conscious Unique Self, living in the largest evolutionary context, giving your gifts with devotion to heal and transform not only your personal sphere but, ultimately, the whole world.

Success 3.0 is to fully embody the unique life that is yours to live and fully give the gifts that are yours to give from a place of the most expanded state and the highest structure-stage of enlightened consciousness.

When you fully wake up, grow up and show up, the evolutionary impulse incarnates as you. You become an expression of radical personal intimacy and evolutionary creativity. You embody a purpose-driven and values-driven life, overflowing with aliveness, love and energy.

Marc Gafni and Kate Maloney
Success 3.0 Summit
Boulder, Colorado 2014

FOREWORD
BY KEN WILBER

DR. MARC GAFNI'S INTERGRAL UNIQUE SELF TEACHING IS SEMINAL. What you hold in your hands is a radically exciting and ground-breaking book that will change forever not only how you think about enlightenment, but how you understand, from a post-metaphysical perspective, the very nature of human life itself. The Unique Self work is magnificent, and it belongs among the "great books." It offers what may arguably be one of the most significant contemporary evolutions of enlightenment teaching. Unique Self brings together East and West in a higher integral embrace of stunning implications. Unique Self is a pivotal step toward an authentic enlightenment.

The teaching in this book has been evolved primarily by Marc Gafni for over three decades and draws from his own realization, insight, and the enlightenment lineage in which he stands. In Gafni's reading of this lineage, brilliantly articulated in his two-volume opus, *Radical Kabbalah: The Enlightenment Teaching of Unique Self, Nondual Humanism and the Wisdom of Solomon*, which I read in several highly excited nights, Unique Self is a nondual realization of Unique Perspective. This realization expresses itself both as the Unique Perspective on a text and as the Unique Perspective of the realized individual—what Gafni terms, in Lainer's thought, the Judah Archetype, whose perspective is a unique incarnation of unmediated divinity and therefore overrides all previous text, including even the Torah itself. In essence, the realized individual, whose True Self has been disclosed, expresses that True Self through his or her Unique Perspective—what Gafni originally termed "Unique Self." Hence, what Gafni calls the nondual humanism of Unique Self is rooted in this equation, in my wording: True Self + Perspective = Unique Self.

Unique Self brilliantly articulates the idea that within each of us is a postegoic nondual realization of Unique Perspective, a unique incarnation of unmediated divinity. The Unique Self re-inhabits all the natural capacities of the human body-mind and all its multiple intelligences. It embraces its capacity for math, for music, for introspection, for love and interpersonal connection—all the talents and capacities given to human beings—without dismissing the True Self, the One Spirit condition that connects us all. Unique Self drenches and permeates the entire system of what is known as Eastern and Western forms of enlightenment.

The full crystallization of this New Enlightenment/Unique Self teaching that Dr. Gafni initiated, in which he and I have partnered, emerged through a series of many important dialogues that we had over nearly a decade. Through these dialogues, a highly significant new chapter in Integral Theory has emerged. These conversations were coupled with intensive discourse that Marc and I had with other leading Integral spiritual teachers and thinkers, including, initially, Diane Hamilton in a catalytic role and later Sally Kempton. World Spirituality based on Integral principles is an entirely new lineage—a trans-path path. Unique Self models the emergent World Spirituality based on integral principles in that it includes all the good stuff of previous paths, but adds a whole new level of emergence. *And that is something that is extraordinary, historic, and not to be denied.*

FOREWORD
BY BARBARA
MARX HUBBARD

DEEP FROM THE HEART OF THE COSMOS comes the signal: be born as the universe in person! Manifest cosmogenesis as your own divine expression of creation. Bring cosmogenesis—the evolution of the cosmos—into form as you, as co-creators of a new culture in which each human being is an expression of the Impulse of Creation.

In *Your Unique Self* Marc Gafni speaks for the evolutionary impulse during our time of radical shift on Earth from one form of growth, one form of self, one form of species, and one form of society to the next. He speaks for the culture of co-creators, each of us as a Unique Self, a divine expression of the Creator creating.

With great erudition and sensitivity to all the major traditions of the past, he offers us a new Source Code for the evolution of our species, a vital mimetic code to guide us forward.

If you want to be excited, if you yearn to experience the reality of your divine destiny, read this book! Live this book! Write this book into your life. It urges you to shine on the God force AS YOU.

I love this book. It affirms everything I have worked toward all my life. I have been writing lines of this book in 185 volumes of journal since the age of 18. It is the deepening my own discovery of *Conscious* Evolution. We are living through the evolution of evolution itself. The great breakthrough in the 13.8 billion years of evolution, in this labor of love, is that evolution has become conscious of itself in and as us, Unique Selves.

The crises we are facing on Earth are evolutionary drivers awakening in us the Unique Self. When we infuse the rapidly growing genius of human capacity to understand nature's processes of creation—the atom, the gene, the brain, our sciences and technology, with evolutionary love, with *teleros*, the love of higher purpose, what do we see? We see the birth of an emerging species. A universal humanity born into a universe of billions of other planets, just opening our collective eyes.

Let us *con-celebrate* with Life the great privilege of being born at this crossover point from Homo sapiens sapiens to Homo Co-creator. Thank you Marc, for inspiring us to find the way.

PREFACE

WHEN I WAS SIXTEEN, my teacher at seminary school, Pinky Bak, died. I was very close to him. Pinky was for me somewhat of a cross between a big brother and surrogate father. I came from a painful first thirteen years of life, and he felt who I was beyond the trauma. He said to me, "You have gifts to give. Your life is valuable. You are needed." He was the first one who invited me to believe in the possibility of possibility.

Pinky was thirty-two when he died. He fell down right next to me in the middle of a rollicking religious holiday party. As was his custom, he was dancing like a wild man—ecstatic, alive, on fire, and contagious. He half looked up for a moment and said, "Go on without me. I will get up in a second." He then died instantly of a brain aneurysm.

I was numbed with shock and my heart was broken. Later that week, the dean of the school asked me to give the eulogy on behalf of the student body, because everybody knew that I was very close to Pinky. The auditorium was packed. I was lost in grief because my teacher had died, and scared out of my mind because I had never talked in public before. But as I walked up to the podium, something happened. It was like a window from heaven had opened up. In my talk, the words flowed out effortlessly from a place beyond me. They felt like wings, lifting and falling, carrying us all to a place where pain was not king, and broken hearts were healed. I spontaneously promised —not knowing where the words had come from— to pick up the baton that Pinky had dropped, to become a teacher of wisdom in the world. It was done.

The place was silent when I finished. Not silence of absence, when there are no words left to cover over the emptiness. Rather, it was Silence of Presence, when words are insufficient to hold the fullness of a moment. Although at the time I could not name the quality, this was my first genuine experience of Eros, of not only praying to or beseeching God, but also of knowing that I was part of, not separate from, the larger divine field. In a moment of Eros, what I call in this book the Unique Self had shown its face. My Unique Self had shown its face. As it often does, it had made itself known in a peak moment.

And so began, at age sixteen, my calling as a teacher. As is often the case, however, my ego then partially hijacked my Unique Self revelation. I was, on the one hand, sincerely committed to teaching, sharing, and even evolving the wisdom of my lineage, but mixed with that sincere and sacred intention was an egoic need that used my speaking and teaching skill to cover up an aching emptiness. My childhood pain had not been healed or addressed. Instead, I had contained it, tucked it away in some supposedly safe place. This, I believed, was what a good person is supposed to do. I barely remembered where I had stored the container.

So public speaking and teaching, for which I had a gift, welled up from mixed places in my consciousness— from a pure instinct to express the good, but also from an isolated, vulnerable ego, passionately yearning for the wave of embrace and affirmation that came from the public's response to my teaching. At that point in my life, my need for a home and for the aliveness of public recognition unconsciously affected key decisions I made, but in very disguised and subtle ways. The good and sincere intention was so strong that I did not detect the ego's bad advice insinuating itself.

My false core sentence at the time was probably "I am not safe." Your false core initially emerges to cover the pain of alienation and the shock of apparent separation. You then develop a false self to soothe the pain of the false core. The false self is precisely the personality that you unconsciously deploy to hide, deny, or fix your false core. The paradox of the false self is that it usually reflects much that is true about you. The problem is that—at least in part—the false self is motivated by the ego's neediness and not by the authenticity of your Unique Self. The false self is false in the sense that it is not sufficiently motivated by the deeper truth of your own gorgeous and authentic being.

So if my false core sentence was "I am not safe," then my false self at that time probably sounded something like this:

> I am a rabbi, committed to outreach to unaffiliated Jews. I am filled with love, passionately committed, creative, and brilliant. I give my life to God. I serve my

people and the tradition. Everyone is beautiful. I am committed to seeing only the beauty in people. If I just love people enough, I can do anything and take care of anything that comes my way. If I love people, they will feel loved by God. No one could possibly betray or distort my love.

Of course, none of this was fully articulated or even conscious. My false self was true, partially. But it was clouded by the ego's neediness.

I was asleep.

Part of what kept me asleep was—paradoxically—the depth of the teaching, the sincerity of my intention, and my sense of the innate goodness of others and myself. All of this was real, but it was happening at an early stage of egoic unfolding, when I was still, at least in part, identified with my false self. Since part of my energy was running in a false-self track, it ultimately could not sustain itself. The false self may well be telling the truth about your beliefs and intentions. But since it rests on top, and is motivated to hide, deny, or heal the false core sentence "I am not safe," it never connects with the ground of your being and is therefore never stable or secure. I was headed for a series of dramatic train wrecks, with no idea that they were coming.

Evolution beyond Ego

In order to genuinely move beyond ego, beyond the false self—or even more precisely, beyond exclusive identification with ego—you need authentic and sustained contact with the transcendent, with the intention of facilitating your own evolution. You also need rigorous and unflinching self-inquiry, which includes some process of sustained shadow work. Prayer, chanting, contemplative study, and meditation are part of the path. In my early years, as for many young teachers, they were my entire path. But beware of parts pretending to be wholes. These paths may not be enough for you. They were not enough for me.

As I moved from my twenties to late thirties, my separate egoic self began to clarify through a mixture of chant, intense sacred study, and deep pain. By my early forties, the clarification process was becoming more intense and dramatic. But I still was not sufficiently clarified in the full realization of my enlightened Unique Self. Events then took place in my life of such pain and proportion that I almost died of heartbreak.

My own genuine mistakes and misjudgments provided a plausible cover to enable betrayal, public distortion, falsification, power plays, and behind-the-scenes malice. Whatever was not clarified in my person gave a hook to the projections of others, and my world came tumbling down. Held in the burning furnace of personal attacks and public humiliation, by grace, I somehow remained alive. But for a full year, I could barely breathe. Not more than a half hour would go by without my heart welling up with tears. I was not able to utter words of prayer. Only with great pain could I chant, and that very rarely. The visceral heaviness of my heart virtually stopped my life force several times a day. Enduring the pain of sudden rupture from all I held dear, and the insanity of *National Enquirer*-like poisonous lies on the internet, for which there is little recourse, were more than the small egoic self of Marc Gafni could hold. The only analogy I can think of that holds the pain of that time is something like the pain of losing the ones closest to you and then being falsely accused of their murder.

All of this came together as a gift of terrible grace.

I was forced to fully step out of my story. Out of my pseudo story. Out of my ego. Out of my small self. It was simply too painful a place to live.

All the spiritual work of the past twenty-five years came to my aid. But it was a grace, known by many names, that shattered all vessels and cracked me open to a new level of light and love.

For the first time in my life, I found a place inside of me in which it was totally OK if I never taught again. I was able to locate myself outside of my gifts. I did not even know if I would be able to keep them. I was so cracked open that, for a long period of time, sitting in a rocking chair on the porch of some small house seemed like pure bliss. Pain, moments of loving, involvement in details of the world, spaciousness, taking refuge in the Buddha, and flashes of intense enlightened awareness all burst in at regular intervals, always expanding and often dissolving my small self into profound ecstasy.

This went on for almost three years. And as time passed, the vessel expanded. I spent many hours in the first year after the tragedy reading Psalms, by myself or together with my friend Dalit. "Reading" is not quite the right word for what I did. It was more like intense wracked sobbing while reading the text as prayer.

I felt the psalmist and his God close to me, holding me, understanding it all, and lifting me up. And the gifts came back. At some point, I began teaching again, but from a more spacious place, a wider place. The meeting with nonexistence had worked me. The knot of the heart had been untied.

Yet it is not over. Knots can tangle up again very quickly. I untie the knots every day anew.

Something, however, had shifted in a way that is virtually indescribable. It was, on the one hand, slight, modest, small, almost unnoticeable. And yet it was everything, All-That-Is—grand and glorious beyond imagination.

I had experienced in a new way the depth of transformation that is possible when the ego opens up in sweet surrender to the luminous love-light of the One. Only then, after stepping beyond identification with ego—or more accurately, being thrown out of ego—was I able to take the next step. To truly live from source as Unique Self, passionately committed to evolutionary manifestation, yet increasingly unattached to the results of my effort. There was no choice. There is never really a choice.

So how do you live as Source? How do you allow your self to be lived by love as a force for healing and transformation? Not by leaving your story behind, but by entering the full depth of your story. Not your ego story—but your Unique Self story. It is on this essential distinction that your enlightenment and very life pivot.

This book speaks dangerous words. Dangerous to your sense that you are small; to your feeling that you are alone and invisible; to your belief that you are worthless, inadequate, or bad; to your belief that you are too much or not enough.

I invite you to listen dangerously.

As William Blake writes, "no bird soars too high if he soars with his own wings." What it means to soar with your own wings is the new enlightenment teaching of Unique Self, which I am honored to transmit to you in these pages.

CHAPTER ONE

THE GREAT INVITATION OF YOUR LIFE

EVERYONE IS RESPONSIBLE for their own awakening. In the same way, every generation is responsible for its own evolution of consciousness. Each generation commits to contribute its own unique insights to the ongoing transformation and evolution of consciousness. At its core, consciousness is love—the evolution of consciousness is therefore nothing less than the evolution of love. If you then realize that God is synonymous with love, you begin to understand that the evolution of love is no less than the evolution of God. God is the infinite. The infinite is the intimate. God is the infinity of intimacy.

To be awake is to be a lover: alive, aflame, and open as love.

Therefore, at its heart, to be a lover means to be willing to participate in the transformation of consciousness.

Consciousness = Love = God = Intimacy

I come from a tradition of evolutionary mysticism. Evolution is the creative impulse inherent in the cosmos, to unfold toward ever-higher levels of complexity, consciousness and goodness. The great teaching of my mystical lineage, confirmed by my own realization, is that the motive force of evolution is love. To awaken is to know that, as Dante put it, love moves the sun and other stars. As the new biology and physics are beginning to implicitly suggest, love is the interior cosmic force that animates and drives the evolutionary impulse. Love is the strange attractor, the allurement that holds the universe together. Alfred North Whitehead said that evolution is really the gentle movement toward God by the gentle persuasion of love[1]—and sometimes far from gentle.

This book intends to unfold the teaching of Unique Self. What is your Unique Self? Unique Self is the individualized expression of the love-intelligence that lives as you. To realize your Unique Self then is your contribution, your gift, to the evolution of love which is no less than the evolution of God.

Awakening to your Unique Self is the change that changes everything. Aligning with your Unique Self fundamentally shifts your worldview, your purpose, and your internal experience of your self, your relationships, your sexuality, your shadow, and the way you love. Unique Self enlightenment relocates you in a larger evolutionary context. It enacts in you new leadership ability, and fosters your capacity to form relationships that are both unique and evolutionary.

This is not a book of spiritual information. Instead, it is designed to give you a transmission that can shift your consciousness. This shift can bring many gifts to your life and make you a gift to the life of All-That-Is.

You could keep your distance and read from a safe place. Or you could say, "I am here. I am ready to undergo a momentous leap in my own personal evolution. I am willing to engage in the work of self-creation. I am ready for a transformation of identity. I am ready to leave my small self behind. I am ready to recognize my True Self, incarnate my Unique Self and live as the evolutionary force of love."

To awaken to your Unique Self is to be lived as God, which, in truth, means to be lived as love. This book is an invitation for you to understand, realize and practice Unique Self in the story of your life—for all of this is just words, until we learn it in the stories of our own lives.

CHAPTER TWO

THE NEW ENLIGHTENMENT OF UNIQUE SELF

WHAT DO WE MEAN BY UNIQUE SELF? Your Unique Self is not ego or personality. It is the essence that lies beneath and beyond your personality. It is the unique God-spark living in you and as you. Your Unique Self is the infinite love-intelligence—the All-That-Is—living in you, as you, and through you.[1] The higher your level of consciousness, the more fully you are able to realize your Unique Self.

Unique Self is revealed and realized throughout your life in moments of flow and grace, regardless of your level of consciousness. Yet it is only after you have begun to move past the grasping of your separate self ego, and realized your nature as indivisible from the infinite, that your Unique Self is revealed as the full and stable realization of your enlightenment.

In other words, there's a process involved in the new enlightenment of Unique Self. You first realize that you are part of the seamless coat of the Universe. You then realize that the Universe is seamless but not featureless—and that you are one of its essential features.[2] You see that you are irreducibly unique, and therefore irreplaceable as a unique expression of All-That-Is. You realize that your personal existence, your being, is utterly distinct, worthy, and needed.

Unique Self is the enlightened realization that you are both absolutely one with the whole, and absolutely unique. Realizing your Unique Self will fundamentally change the way you understand virtually every facet of your awakened life. Once we've engaged the core teachings of Unique Self, we will look separately at how these teachings fundamentally reconfigure and dramatically re-vision our understanding of love, joy, shadow, sexuality, parenting, death, relationships, loneliness, and spirituality.

Are you ready to respond to this invitation, to offer yourself to the infinite love-intelligence that wants desperately to show up in the world through and as you?

Then keep on reading . . .

Being God's Verb

You are God's verb. To be God's verb, you only need to leave your identification with your small-self ego behind. You will then be able to identify with the unlimited and unfathomable mind of God, coming into its own by manifesting through and as you.

Are you tired of feeling trapped in the maze of your own self-contraction? Are you tired of your constant reaction, which creates your constant contraction? Are you tired of feeling like little more than a living cluster of habits and preconditioned reactions? Or are you here to survive in your physical body? I hope not, because you will not. Or to get rich or get famous? I hope not, because as mama said, "You can't take it with you."

You are here to be the poem that only you can be. You are here to sing the song that only you can sing. You are here to be the unique presence in the world that no one else but you can be.

God Is Having a "You" Experience

When I live my Unique Self, then God is having a Marc experience. When my oldest son lives his Unique Self, then God is having an Eytan experience. The same is true for you. When you live your Unique Self, God is having a "you" experience. God is devastated when Marc, instead of living the great mythic story of Marc, tries to be John or Rob.

False Self and True Self

All the great traditions tell us about two selves: a "true" self, and a "false" or "fallen" self. Your everyday ordinary self is known as the separate self. Your false self is a distorted or unhealthy expression of your separate self. This might involve a distorted self-understanding due to false core sentences or belief structures. For example, "I'm not safe," "I'm not good," or "I'm not enough" are false core sentences that unconsciously filter our perception of reality.[3]

Even after we clarify the distortion of our false self and access our healthy separate self, a fundamental distortion still remains in place. This distortion is the illusion that our separate self is all that we are. From this perspective, our separate self is also our false self in that it is our limited identity with our personality or ego—it is the cluster of needs, drives, memories, fears, and expectations that you typically refer to as "me." It is a painfully finite self, born into the illusion of separation. It is a life cast in shadows, like a prisoner in Plato's cave.[4]

But while your false self is trapped in time and therefore destined to die, your True Self is eternal. It is the infinite Spirit within, the effortless expanse of awareness behind all your experiences. It is forever unblemished by the pains and ecstasies of time, for it exists completely outside of time.

The overall number of True Selves in the Universe is one. Whenever someone realizes their True Self, that person is literally in a state of at-one-ment, communing with the infinite singularity of being. There is only one. However—and this is the central realization of Unique Self—The One True Self shows up differently through every pair of eyes. In the old enlightenment, True Self was understood to erase all distinction. In the New Enlightenment, we realize that enlightenment always has a perspective.[5]

Human beings used to think we were directly engaging reality as it is. This is why every spiritual system thought that it owned the truth, that it was seeing reality itself. But this was only partially true. At some point, we began to realize that there is no reality without perspective. To put it another way, reality itself is fundamentally constructed from perspectives.[6]

In the old, dominant paradigm, we assumed that perception was a faculty that showed each of us the same picture and revealed the true nature of things. In the new paradigm, we understand that our perspective is like a pair of glasses through which our vision takes place. Wear red-tinted glasses, and the world is bathed in red. Wear Christian-tinted glasses, and see Jesus in your meditations. Wear Hindu-tinted glasses, and see Shiva or Kali in your meditations. Wear Buddhist glasses, and see everything as empty. Wear Jewish-tinted glasses, and see all of reality as an apparition of the *Shekhinah*.

The recognition that every culture—and indeed every individual—holds a unique perception of the world is an evolutionary emergent.[7] Our conclusion, however, is not that of the postmodern deconstructive thinkers who were among the champions of this insight. Deconstruction wrongly assumed that when perspective is revealed to be part of the process of meaning making, there is no longer any real meaning. On the contrary, when we understand perspective, we understand that every culture and every great tradition of spirit has its own unique perspective which reveals a plenitude of meaning and not a dearth or death of meaning. All cultures perceive essence, but each Unique Perspective gives a particular resonance and cast to essence. Loyalty to one's religion and culture is not, therefore (as modern and postmodern fashions sometimes suggest) primitive or fundamentalist. It is rather partially true, in that it is how my culture is intuiting essence. The premodern mistake was the failure to realize that every religion has a particular perspective, and therefore not to realize that no religion can claim that its intuition of ultimate truth is the only truth. Now that we understand that every great tradition and culture perceives essence through a particular perspective, we can avoid the tragic mistake of deconstructing the traditions as meaningless. Instead, we understand that every tradition plays a particular instrument in the symphony of spirit that is indeed making sacred music. All of the perspectives come together to create a symphony.

Unique Self Enlightenment

Your Unique Self expresses itself in your drive to reach your limitless potential. It is your authentic desire to move beyond your exclusive identification with your small self, and to realize something within you that is both unique to you and infinitely larger than you. In this process, the first step is to dis-identify with your small self, your ego, and identify with the larger field of existence. You understand that you are part of a larger whole.

The ego tends to identify all that you are with your body-mind personality. It's like the story of the biker who irrationally picked a fight with someone who touched his bike. When pressed afterward to explain himself, he said, "When you touch my bike, you touch me." This is precisely the overreach of your ego when it claims to be the fullness of your identity. In this sense, the ego is an expression of your false self.

Classically, enlightenment is the move from false self to True Self. The motivation to dis-identify with your egoic false self is the evolutionary impulse of love.[8]

Evolutionary love is not an emotion but a perception.[9] It is the capacity that allows you to perceive your own true nature as far more vast, stunning, and spacious than your "skin-encapsulated ego." Love realizes that your small self is not isolated, alienated, and alone—it is a spark in the inferno of love and evolving consciousness that we sometimes call God.

It is the force of evolutionary love that drives you to *trance-end* your separate egoic self and move toward union with the whole.

However, the realization that your separate self is one with the whole is a stage on the journey, not its endpoint. The new enlightenment moves one crucial step beyond classic enlightenment. In the new enlightenment, you realize that the spark is not merely absorbed in the larger light. Even as the spark dances in the roaring flames of heart-melting and searing divinity, it does not lose its unique character. As identification with separate self disappears, your clarified individuality, your Unique Self, appears. This is the new enlightenment of Unique Self.

Enlightenment has a perspective.
Your perspective.
Your Unique Self.

CHAPTER THREE

TWO VISIONS OF ENLIGHTENMENT

THROUGHOUT HISTORY, when the sages and mystic philosophers looked at consciousness, two very different understandings about the self have contended with each other for dominance. Each has termed its understanding of the self "enlightened." The first conception is that of classical mystical consciousness. This view understands the separate self—or ego—as being essentially false and the source of suffering, while proclaiming impersonal consciousness (often called True Self, or inner self) to be the essence of your True Nature or identity.

While this view is often correctly identified with classical nondual Eastern teaching, it is not limited by geography. True Self has gone by many signifiers, including *rigpa* in Tibetan Buddhism, *mochin degadlut*, or Expanded Mind in Kabbalah, *antar atman* (inner self) or *tat* (That, as in the aphorism *tat tvam asi* "Thou Art That") in Hinduism, and Christ Consciousness in Christianity. This realization of the True Nature of self is what is classically termed "enlightenment." It has also been called self-realization (Shankara, Abulafia), Liberation (Ramana Maharshi), or being awake, the state the Buddha famously attained under the Bodhi tree. This understanding about the True Nature of self that I am calling "classical enlightenment" is indeed true.[1] But it is also partial.

The second understanding, which also calls itself enlightened, makes almost the directly opposite claim. This teaching, which flowered in the

West during the so-called Age of Enlightenment in the mid-eighteenth century, asserts that your personal, separate self—your identity as a distinct individual—is your essential nature. This is seen by Western enlightenment thinkers such as Hobbes, Locke, and Rousseau as the basis of all human rights and responsibilities. Thus, the Western enlightenment conception sees the failure to recognize the autonomy of each individual as the source of all suffering. This is the core understanding behind almost all of Western psychology.

The understanding of self as the large, impersonal ground of Being suggested by mysticism is either ignored, denied, or deemed irrelevant and even immoral by the Western enlightenment conception. As with the nondual understanding of the self, the Western enlightenment conception is true but partial.

The recognition of Unique Self transcends and includes the true but partial insights of both visions of enlightenment, and for the first time in the history of consciousness allows a higher Integral embrace of both.[2] In Unique Self enlightenment, you recognize and realize your nature as indivisible from the larger field of consciousness, even as you know yourself to be an absolute unique expression of True Self, unlike any other. True Self always looks out through a unique set of eyes, which reveals a radically one-of-a-kind and special perspective. But not only a unique perspective. You also have a unique taste. Your unique taste is the unique quality of intimacy that is yours and yours alone. The intimate quality of reality appears uniquely as the taste of you. That is what it means to be the personal face of essence. You personal quality is not merely your separate-self personality. Rather your personal quality is a combination of the unique perspective and unique taste of your True Self. In this way, you transcend the limitation of separate self while affirming the autonomy, value, and infinite dignity of your Unique Self.

True Self + Perspective + Taste = Unique Self[3]

Two Images of Light

In the old scientific paradigm, light was thought to be of one quality and nature. In the old paradigm of awakening, to be enlightened was to be absorbed in the unqualified field of light, which is one. In the new science paradigm, we realize that every beam of light vibrates at its own unique frequency. To be enlightened, then, means to consciously live the radiance and purpose of your singularly unique frequency of light. This is the core teaching of the Unique Self enlightenment.

Classical enlightenment, the old enlightenment, viewed uniqueness as the enemy. The belief was that your experience of uniqueness would obscure the realization of your identity with All-That-Is; That ego or separate self is something to be surrendered, pushed aside, utterly dissolved in the timeless Absolute. There is an element of truth to this—the ego must be *trance-ended*. You must end the trance of the ego.

You will always experience yourself in part as a separate self—that is as it should be. If you did not, you would be psychotic or otherwise deranged. What you need to transcend is your exclusive identification with your egoic separate self—which creates the sense of suffocation, fear, and drabness that may pass as your life. This fundamental error in identity is the root of virtually all suffering. Your disconnection from your larger context, and the aliveness it holds for you, gives birth to every form of egoic grasping and addiction.

But the ego contains within it more than a glimmer of truth. As we'll see later, the ego bears gifts that require clarification.

Clarification takes place through contact with the transcendent, resulting in the revelation of the larger whole of which the separate-self ego is but a part. The gifts of the ego, which are the intimations of your infinitely valuable uniqueness, can then flower in your higher realization as Unique Self. We must love and nourish our egos, not destroy them altogether. Ego prefigures and points toward Unique Self.

Once you can transcend exclusive identification with ego and celebrate your Unique Self, you are at the portal to your full enlightenment. Once you shatter the tyranny of the ego's dream, even as you awaken to your unique calling of radical love, beauty, and obligation, you begin to live as Source, naturally manifesting your deepest authentic desire.

Your Unique Self is your birthright. In your Unique Self, you begin to live as Source, carrying the evolution of love and the transformation of consciousness one generation forward. It is from this place that you discover your ultimate purpose in living, where you remember your most sacred vows, taken long before you were even born—promising to bring as much love and light as you possibly can to a world that is so desperately in need of your extraordinary gifts.

The Biology of Unique Self

Unique Self expresses itself in all dimensions of reality. It begins at the base atomic level of matter, or what the Buddhists call form: "Physical atoms each have their own specific energy signature. Similarly, assemblies of atoms radiate their own identifying energy patterns. So every material structure in the universe, including you and me, radiates a unique energy signature."[4] And, "Each atom is unique, because the distribution of its positive and negative charges coupled with its spin rate generates a specific vibration or energy pattern."[5] Ascending the great chain of being from matter to body, we come to what we might call the biology of Unique Self. To be clear, I am not suggesting that this is evidence of the enlightenment teaching of Unique Self in the formal sense. Rather, it suggests an expression of Unique Self on a biological level. Human beings used to think that consciousness was a higher level of reality than the material plane of matter. We now realize that this is not quite true. It is more accurate to say that every human event has an interior and exterior face, an inside and an outside expression. The outside viewed through the third-person mechanisms of science and empirical verification is matter. The inside, accessed through introspection and other forms of internally directed forms of knowing, is consciousness.

So we would naturally expect uniqueness, which appears at the interior level as the awakening of your unique consciousness, to also appear at the exterior plane, the level of form. Looking specifically at biology, we see that of course uniqueness does appear in biology in highly dramatic and unmistakable ways. Every single human being is biologically unique, with a unique molecular and cellular signature.

Clearly, uniqueness from this biological perspective is much more than mere social or psychological conditioning. Rather, uniqueness is the cellular reality of life.

The evolutionary realization that the core structures of Unique Self are rooted in the very cellular level of human being-ness suggests that Unique Self is not merely an elite expression of enlightenment, but is, at least in potential, an awakening that is possible for every human being. This is but one more indication that it is time for a radical democratization of enlightenment.

The Democratization of Enlightenment

It used to be that enlightened living was for the elite. The few great lovers, saints, and sages throughout history reminded us that something more was possible, that there was a better way to live, that joy and overflowing love could and did exist as the animating essence of everyday life.

This tiny elite of subtle and evolved minds and hearts held alive for all of us the possibility that human beings could genuinely realize a transformation of identity, that they could truly evolve from their small constricted egos into spacious, dynamic, enlightened beings.

In days gone by, we relied on this elite to guide our world. Today, that age has passed. The old elite no longer has the power to guide us. We can no longer hope that in some room somewhere, in the halls of spiritual power or the inner chambers of an ashram or temple, there are holy, wise people upon whom we can rely for our salvation.

In a globally interconnected world, one person acting alone or a small group of ignorant individuals has the ability to literally destroy humanity. The lesson is clear. For better and for worse, the age of ruling elites, be they spiritual or political, is over. Democracy is the evolutionary unfolding in our era. It began with the democratization of governments. Now it must move to the democratization of enlightenment. This is the enlightenment of True Self beyond personality and ego, which then expresses itself in the full glory and power of Unique Self.

Enlightenment is a genuine possibility, and therefore a sacred obligation, for every single person. You are not obligated from without. You are obligated in love by your own highest possibility.[6]

The disciples of one master liked to explain this radical Unique Self principle with a story:

> A precocious child was convinced that the king was not as wise as people claimed. And so he set out—as young people are wont to do—to prove his point. He came before the king with a question. "Sire," he said with great audacity, "it is said that you know the future and can answer any question posed. Well, I have a question for you." The assembled court gasped at his insolence. But the boy went on. "I have in my closed hand a butterfly, sire. Tell me, is it alive or dead?"
>
> The boy thought to himself, "if he says 'alive,' I will simply squeeze and kill it, and if he says 'dead,' then I will open my hand and let it fly away."
>
> The sage was silent for a moment, even as the room grew very silent. When he finally spoke, it was with the

gentlest voice the boy had ever heard. "My son," said the king, "whether the butterfly lives or dies depends on you."

It depends on us. On each and every one of us uniquely.

Answering the Call

Once you understand at the very cellular level of your being that your uniqueness is not a historical accident but an intentional expression of essence, then you realize that enlightenment is a genuine option for every human being—including you! The living universe took 13.7 billion years of intentional evolution to manifest the new and original evolutionary potential of your Unique Self. When you realize this, everything in your essential experience of life changes.

Once you understand that your uniqueness is not the haphazard result of your cultural, social or psychological conditioning, but that all of these are necessary conditions for the emergence of the personal face of essence that is you, your essential experience of life transforms. You move from having a desperate need to escape your life to the radical embrace of your life.

When this happens, fate is transformed to destiny. Desperation becomes celebration. Grasping becomes purposeful action and resignation becomes activism. The contracted smallness of your frightened suffering self becomes the expanded joyful realization of your Unique Self. At such times, you know that the irreducible uniqueness of every awakened human being is a sign that reality actually invites, and even lovingly demands, your enlightenment. Reality yearns for a full and authentic expression of your uniqueness, for you to live in the world as God's verb.

It is from this place that you answer the call of Unique Self. It is from this place that you give the world your desperately needed unique gifts, those charismatic endowments that arise from your Unique Self. This is what it means to answer the call.

Unique Self enlightenment is a genuine possibility and therefore a responsibility for every human being. So, we could say that failure to clarify the contours of your Unique Self is not a failure of the contracted ego but a failure to love God. For to love God is to let God see through your eyes—through the unique perspective of essence which is you.

Your obligation and joy in being alive is to clarify your unique perspective, realize your Unique Self and give your unique gift. This is how you answer the call. Democratization of enlightenment, therefore, does not mean that everyone is enlightened, but rather that a full expression of authentic unique essence is a genuine possibility and therefore a genuine expression of love-obligation for every living being. In other words, awakening to your Unique Self is the joy and responsibility of answering the call.

Enlightenment Is Sanity

The future of our world depends on your enlightenment. A genuine shift in your consciousness will affect a similar shift in the consciousness of many of the people with whom you come into contact, and will spread enlightenment in ever-widening circles. The ease and urgency of enlightenment is contagious and exhilarating.

Enlightenment means no more and no less than sanity. To be enlightened is to know reality. To know reality is to be sane. The core of your reality is your identity. A correct understanding of your identity is critical to your sanity and joy.

If to be enlightened means to be sane: so-called normal consciousness is insane. "Normal" consciousness rooted in the grasping ego produces suffering. "Normal" consciousness killed 100 million people in the last century. That is not normal. To be sane is to be in right relationship with yourself and with all of the larger frameworks and contexts in which your Unique Self lives and breathes.

One of the simplest definitions of sanity used in the psychological literature is to know who you are. To be sane is to know your identity, to recognize your name. For example, if I tell you that my name is Ken Wilber when my name is really Marc Gafni and I insist on being called Ken Wilber, there is a fairly good chance that I am more than a bit insane. Clearly, I don't know my true identity.

But the distance between the identity of Marc and Ken may be less wide than the distance between my experience of myself as a separate, skin-encapsulated ego-self, and the experience of my True Self. From the place of True Self, I am able to access much more than my limited personal power, knowing, creativity and love. Rather, all of the power, knowing, creativity and love in the universe flow through me. When I see from the place of True Self, there is no reason for me to be jealous of you, to lash out at you or to do anything other then love you as myself. In some sense, you are myself.

So here is the great question: If enlightenment is so great, why isn't everyone seeking it? If enlightenment is the answer to our suffering, if it actually delivers on all of its wildly amazing promises—which it does— why is the world not lining up for intensive enlightenment studies?

Some enlightenment teachers explain that this is because of the clever obfuscations of the ego, which does everything in its power to avoid its own death. In other words, since the ego doesn't want to die, it attaches you to a narrow identity as a small self. Other teachers say that the work required to liberate into True Self beyond ego is simply too demanding for most people. Still other teachers may blame the seductions of culture and society, which so entice you with their pseudo-comforts that it is hard to free yourself from the game.

All of these explanations certainly carry some weight. But the problem is not with the seekers of enlightenment. Instead, there is a defect in the way classical enlightenment is being presented.

The teaching of classical enlightenment often points to a state that, at its core, appears boring, dislocating and alienating. It is dislocating because it leads a student to ask, quite rightly, "If I give up my separate self-ego identity, then who am I?" Many enlightenment teachers respond to this natural question by pointing out that it comes from the voice of the ego. In other words, they imply that once you're enlightened, it doesn't even arise. The price for enlightenment, as they say in the Zen tradition, is "Die to separate self!"

In one sense, that is true, but it is also partial. If enlightenment meant only disappearing into the undifferentiated oneness of True Self, it would seem to deny the sacred dignity of the individual. And besides, (as many seekers intuit), it would be boring. The sense of creative edge, vitality and becoming that are the ground of our aliveness would be lost in the being-ness of it all. If, to be enlightened means to lose "me," then it becomes irrelevant to most of the world.

Unique Self enlightenment teaches you how to lose "me" at the level of ego only to reclaim a higher and deeper "me" at the level of Unique Self. The Unique Self enlightenment teaching points out that to be enlightened—to know who you really are, your true identity— is not merely to recognize True Self, rather, Unique Self enlightenment demands that you move beyond your separate self to True Self, while understanding that the realization of True Self is the ground for the awakening of your Unique Self. As an individual, you correctly sense that the source of your dignity and value is your irreducible uniqueness. And, the Unique Self teachings confirm that enlightenment is not a loss of individuality. It is to live at the energized edge of your evolutionary creativity and your capacity for becoming that is both indivisibly part of the greater One, and, at the same time, ecstatically you. This is sanity. This is what it means to live in a larger context as an evolutionary lover. This is enlightenment. This is your true identity. Enlightenment and sanity are one.

To be enlightened means to be in love—sometimes agonizingly, sometimes blissfully—but always in love. To be enlightened means to be living a life of ecstatic expression, aligned obligation, and unique meaning and fulfillment. Enlightenment is the life of pleasure, for the enlightened person knows how to discern between pleasures. There is no greater pleasure, even when painful, than your enlightened life manifesting as your Unique Self.

In Sanskrit, *dharma* means something like "truth," "law," and "path." When you access the truth of Unique Self, the individualized law of your life reveals itself, and the path that is only yours to walk opens up and welcomes you.

When you realize the dharma of Unique Self, your relationship to love, sex, joy, pleasure, relationships, parenting, ethical failures, jealousies, anger, all forms of acting out, death, reincarnation, heartbreak, and the very purpose of your life on Earth will all evolve dramatically.

The Difference between Separateness and Uniqueness

Perhaps the greatest mistake in the evolution of human spirituality was the failure to properly distinguish between separateness and uniqueness. This simple statement is the result of many years of meditation on Unique Self and the reading of countless classic and popular texts that all confused separateness and uniqueness, each in its own way. Once this realization dawned on me, I could see that one of the great intractable problems standing in the face of human evolution could be resolved. The knotted contradiction between the major types of human spirituality are easily unraveled, opening the door to a higher integral embrace of enlightenment. This acknowledgment of the difference between separate and unique in turn allows us to move one vital step closer toward the emergence of a genuine translineage dharma and world spirituality.

The core contradiction lies between the dominant motifs and moods of Eastern and Western spirituality. Each suggests a different path—paths that are, to a large extent, mutually exclusive. Both are right and both are wrong. Or to put it another way, each one has a piece of the story, but each thinks its respective piece is actually the whole story. When a part pretends to be a whole, pathology of some form is invariably produced. Moreover, Eastern and Western spirituality each make a critical mistake based on an essential confusion between separateness and uniqueness.

Each side in this dharma combat, which has spanned the generations, is motivated by pure and holy motives. Each, with its teachings and practices, seeks the highest expression and flowering of human love and goodness. Each, with its teachings and practices, wishes to end suffering. Yet each made the same mistake, in the opposite manner.

The Insight and Mistake of the East

Eastern spirituality, by and large, rightly sees the separate self as an illusion. The realization of this illusion comes from profound spiritual practices like meditation, which work to open the eye of the spirit. Not only is the separate self exposed as an illusion, it is also the root source of most human suffering. Fear, death, terror, and cruelty in virtually all of its forms can ultimately be traced back to the illusion of the separate self. It is for this most powerful and compelling of reasons that the East devoted an enormous amount of energy to dispelling the illusion of the separate-self ego.

In realizing that the separate self is an illusion, the East made a mistake: it confused separateness and uniqueness. The axiomatic assumption in many Eastern teachings—both ancient and modern—is that to transcend the separate self, you must leave behind not only the illusion of separation, but also the experience of uniqueness.

Much effort was directed to demonstrating that what seemed to be unique and particular was in fact common and universal, and what seemed to be personal was actually impersonal. There was great truth in some of this teaching, and it clearly brought immense spiritual depth and some measure of peace to many.

And yet the core teaching did not take root among the masses. The problem was not simply that the masses were lazy, stupid, or in lower states of consciousness, as some teachers told us. The deeper problem was that the masses felt that the teaching violated their basic sense of the necessity, desirability, and dignity of uniqueness. The problem was—and is—that uniqueness just will not go away. The majority of people correctly feel that to surrender their uniqueness would be to surrender their life force, as well as their personal value and dignity. The personal is, by its very nature, *unique*. The dignity and value of the personal derive directly from its uniqueness.

You can have a powerful and authentic experience of your own specialness even after the dissolution of your ego. Many Eastern teachings try valiantly to explain this away by telling you in many different ways that your lingering experience of uniqueness or specialness is merely evidence that you have not yet evolved beyond ego.

But you, and many like you, know in your deepest place that this is simply not true. You experience the reality of your specialness and uniqueness not as an expression of ego, but as a glorious expression of your truest nature. You understand that your uniqueness is the highest expression of God looking out from behind your eyes and taking in your uniquely gorgeous perspective and insight. You must move beyond your separate self, even as you must embrace and affirm your uniqueness beyond ego. Because the East demands that you throw out your uniqueness as part of dispelling the illusion of the ego or the separate self, you correctly rebel against this dharma. You intuitively affirm the value of the personal. To you, impersonality feels like a violation of the very quality of humanness that you hold most dear.

You feel your uniqueness as a deep truth. So you reject the dharma of the East, and while trying to salvage your uniqueness, you cling to your separate self. Ironically, the failure of virtually all Eastern approaches to spirituality to make this essential distinction between uniqueness and separateness undermines the ability of the discerning heart and mind to receive the great dharma of the East. It is for this reason that the Eastern teachings that have been disseminated throughout the Western world have ultimately failed to break out of a very small and elite audience, and have not had a genuinely transformative impact upon mainstream culture.

Of course the East is half right. The illusion of an isolated ego, the separate self, really is the source of virtually all suffering. The confusion between separateness and uniqueness in Eastern teaching has paradoxically caused the rejection of Eastern teaching in the West. The

West has essentially ignored the Eastern call to evolve beyond separate-self ego, and most of humanity has remained stuck with ego and all of its attendant horrors.[7]

The Insight and Mistake of the West

Conventional Western spirituality, like the spirituality of the East, is motivated by love and the desire to end suffering. However, the West came to essentially opposite conclusions about how to achieve this same result. The West saw the affirmation of human individuality as the greatest good of the human spirit. Western spirituality asserted that our rights and relationships are rooted in the dignity of the separate self. It is the separate self that is in relationship not only with others but also with God. Communion with the divine rather than absorption into the One becomes the good of spiritual practice.

It is the great divine gift to affirm human adequacy and dignity through every encounter between humans and God. For humans to be addressed in this encounter, their distinct otherness as a separate self apart from God must be affirmed and supported. In other words, our relationship with God requires some degree of separation. Two parties can only meet in love and mutuality if they are separate. We are both overwhelmed by the presence and at the same time affirmed by the presence as a separate other. In the revelation of the infinite, the finite is held in love, nourished and challenged at the same time. Our individuality becomes the source of our dignity. Moreover, it is in our individuality that we find our ability to love, to act in compassion, and to take responsibility for our destiny.

For one who is wholly merged with the infinite, there is no encounter. If there is no encounter, then there is no love, no dignity, and no responsibility. If there is no other, then we cease to be a moral agent and a lover. With the total annihilation of the personal comes the end of personal responsibility. If human beings are not separate selves with individual rights and responsibilities, then there is neither good nor evil. It becomes virtually impossible to distinguish between what is below and what is beyond. Good and evil imply relationship. When there is an identity of subjects, when humans and God are one, when we are truly submerged in a condition of *tat tvam asi* ("Thou art That"), there can be no relationship. Where there is no relationship, there is no love, no good, and no evil.

The miracle of We comes only from the union of I and Thou. What is love without an I and a Thou? Ethics, goodness, and judgment are meaningful only in the realm of the personal. They have no place in a Universe of no-selves.

For all of these very noble reasons, the West insisted on the reality of the separate self. However, Western spirituality made the same great mistake as the East, but in the opposite direction. The West essentially confused separateness and uniqueness. Western teachers wrongly assumed that all the virtues of love and relationship required the dignity of individuality in the form of a separate self. This is simply not true. All the goods and virtues of love, relationship, compassion, responsibility, and all the rest can be had through the Unique Self. There is absolutely no need for the separate self. The Unique Self, as we have shown, emerges in its full splendor only after the separate self has been transcended. You can experience the full dignity, responsibility, and joy of individuality by recognizing your uniqueness. Uniqueness does not require separateness.

The result of this colossal mistake in Western spirituality has been that your intuitive spiritual desire to evolve beyond exclusive identification with your ego—to transcend your separate self—has been thwarted and even ridiculed by Western spiritual teaching. Your desire to reach for the transpersonal was stymied because it seemed like you needed to reject the personal to get there. The Western deification of the personal blocked the gateways necessary for your enlightenment. Your heart knew this was wrong. You knew you needed to transcend your separate self, but you did not know how to do it without losing the critical moral and relational virtues of the personal. So you remained stuck in the personal, unable to find a path beyond yourself.

For both East and West, drawing a correct distinction between separateness and uniqueness allows for a powerful evolution of their respective teachings. This crucial dharmic distinction allows for a higher and Integral embrace of these seemingly disparate teachings, which split the world of spirit into two warring camps.

The Unique Self is the pivot point for this translineage spiritual breakthrough, which allows for the evolutionary integration of these two teachings.

For the West, the Unique Self is the source of human dignity, love, obligation, and destiny. At the deepest level, you know that your Unique Self is not your separate self. Your separate self is an illusion, though you remain a unique strand in the seamless coat of the Universe. Spiritual practice moves you to realize your essential enmeshment with the larger reality, even as you retain the dignity of your distinction. Uniqueness is the source of this dignity, as well as your sense of intimacy.

For the East, the realization of Unique Self is equally critical. It is precisely the recognition of the Unique Self that allows for the transcendence of the illusion of separate self without the wholesale rejection of individual specialness and uniqueness. You are able to fully embrace the call to evolve beyond separate self and ego, even as you affirm and embrace your Unique Self that emerges from your Buddha nature.

For both the East and the West, higher translineage integration can be achieved. A genuine evolution of spirit can be accomplished. The full glory of meditative realization and classic enlightenment is redeemed and recognized as the first major step. In the second step, the full glory of individual dignity is realized in the postegoic Unique Self.

Are You Special? The Distinction Between Separateness and Uniqueness

One of the most confusing things to people on a genuine spiritual path is the utter denial of specialness. You have an experience that you are special, but spiritual teachers and books tell you that if you experience yourself as special, you are still stuck in ego. So you work really hard to get rid of the feeling of being special. But it is always there, lurking in the corner just beneath the surface. This makes you feel like an impostor and fraud. On the one hand, you are having intense spiritual experiences during regular practice and living your compassion in the world. On the other hand, the lurking feeling of specialness makes you feel like your realization is false and fraudulent. "Special" is often used interchangeably with "unique." To think you are special is to think you are unique, which is radically rejected by most spiritual teachers on the contemporary scene.

One well-known spiritual teacher speaks of what she calls the illusion of uniqueness. She says time and again in her teaching of impersonal enlightenment that there is "no such thing as a unique spiritual experience." This is precisely wrong. The deeper the spiritual experience, the more unique it becomes. Your enlightenment always has a perspective. The very essence of enlightenment is the liberation of your unique perspective from the prison of voices not your own.

A second example of this rejection of specialness as being anti-spiritual is *A Course in Miracles*. Below is a citation from one entry entitled "The Pursuit of Specialness":

> *The pursuit of Specialness*
> *Is always at the cost of peace*
> *You are not Special*
> *If you think you are*
> *And would defend your specialness*
> *Against the truth of what you really are*
> *How can you know the truth*
> *Specialness always makes comparisons*
> *It is established by a lack seen in another*
> *The pursuit of Specialness*
> *Must bring you pain*[8]

The conclusion of the section is that specialness is but an illusion that needs to be forgiven, and dispelled through forgiveness.

A *Course in Miracles* is a significant and profound teaching. And yet in both examples and in the larger teachings that they represent, the same two mistakes are made. First, there is a complete conflation of uniqueness or specialness on the one side, and separateness on the other. They are all taken to refer to the same thing. Now, it is true that the assertion of specialness is one of the favorite tactics through which the consciousness of separate self attempts to ward off the terror of its own inevitable death and dissolution. From this perspective, specialness is indeed an illusion of ego to be overcome in order to gain the peace and joy that come from a realization of your true nature, the realization that you are not separate or alone but an indivisible and eternal expression of the seamless coat of the Universe. However, from a perspective of Unique Self, of course you are special. That is precisely what it means to be a Unique Self. Your utter uniqueness is what makes you special.

The second confusion in the teaching that blithely rejects specialness is the failure to distinguish between different stages on the spiritual path—what are often referred to as levels of consciousness. For example, ego and Unique Self represent two distinct levels of consciousness.

When you are operating from the level of ego, your feeling that "I am special" is the ego's delusion. The ego's feeling that "I am special" is based on something unreal. Seduced by the significance of this truth, enlightenment teachers who stress dis-identification with ego will often mistakenly conflate personal-specialness with ego-specialness, and therefore wrongly reject specialness and personal uniqueness altogether. At the Unique Self, you reconnect to your specialness with the stunning realization: You are special! You are unique!

There are many differences between egoic specialness and Unique Self specialness, which emerges in moments of evolution beyond exclusive identification with ego. But one distinction stands out as a surefire litmus test that will always allow you to distinguish between egoic and Unique Self specialness: specialness at the level of ego is always at someone else's expense. If I am special, that means that others are not. This is the level of ego that *A Course in Miracles* was referring to in saying that specialness exists only by comparison.

However, specialness at the level of Unique Self is of a different order of reality. Unique Self specialness is an authentic realization of overpowering joy. I am special, and so are you. Each of us has a Unique Self. We are not equally talented, wise, sensual, or compassionate. But paradoxically, we are all special, each in our own infinitely unique ways. In the enlightened identification of your uniqueness, you realize your specialness, which is a wondrous and gorgeous expression of your very enlightenment. It is paradoxically this very realization that opens you up to fully perceive and delight in the specialness of others.

Enlightenment Is Not Impersonal

The goal of the New Enlightenment is not impersonal. You do not disappear in your enlightenment. You begin for the first time to appear, for your enlightenment takes on a perspective held for God only by you.

You harbor a greater life than you know. In Unique Self practice, you allow yourself to become available to the extraordinary capacities beyond your imagining that you contain. You gain access to knowing beyond your experience. You are connected to perceptions and practices far beyond the capacity of your small self.

To recognize your unique qualities is simply to be present to what is.

Unique Self is the unique feeling, a personal knowing, of your full presence.

The Personal Face of Essence

Some mystics refer to Unique Self as *ani atzmi*, best translated as "Essential self." Essential is that which is most substantial and real. Essence is what makes something what it is. The wonder of your irreducible uniqueness is your essence.

> *Would that you could*
> *know yourself for a time.*
> *You will be shocked by your delight.*
>
> —Rumi

The Persian poets Rumi and Hafiz wrote their verse to recall you to your essence. Essence is your enlightened state expressed in its unique form. Your Unique Self is not an object. It is the personal face of essence. To realize your essence is to realize your enlightenment. Let yourself be seduced by essence, and your life in all of its passing moments becomes filled with glory.

Unique Self is a direct manifestation of who you are. It is also your gift to the world. Your expression is unique, and if you block it, it will never exist through any other medium. If you do not realize your Unique Self then all that only you can and must offer the world, all that the world needs from you, will be lost.

By accessing your Unique Self, you allow yourself to become available to the extraordinary capacities we each contain. You unleash extra-ordinary possibilities beyond your imagining. You gain access to knowing beyond your experience. It is the individuation of your Unique Self that is the main task of your life.

Too often, people never quite recognize themselves, because they are busy trying to be something or someone else. There is great shock and delight at self-recognition. You are the only perfect expression of what and who you are. So you might as well be yourself. In any event, everyone else is taken.

CHAPTER FOUR

EIGHT STATIONS ON THE ROAD TO UNIQUE SELF

THERE ARE EIGHT DISTINCT STATIONS on the evolutionary path to your Unique Self. You will recognize them as you encounter them on your journey. Let's explore the meanings and contours of the key stations.

Station 1: Pre-personal Self

The first station appears at the beginning of life, before you have developed a sense of your personal separate self. In individual development, this is the station of the infant who is not yet individuated from their mother or environment. However, this pre-personal station doesn't disappear completely after infancy; it remains with us and reappears later in life in different forms. It is, for example, the station of someone who loses their autonomy and sense of identity in an abusive cult or lynch mob or someone caught in the group-think of politically-correct victimology. Falling in love also requires you to move—at least for a time—from the clear boundaries of the personal to the fusion of the pre-personal. It is for this reason that Freud, in his less romantic moments, viewed falling in love as regressive. Deeper insight reveals that this "falling" is an absolutely necessary, if temporary, first station of love. It gives the lover a temporary glimpse into what might be possible.

In the next station, station two, boundaries snap back into place as the personal reasserts itself. This is the station where lovers must decide if they are willing to stay and do the work. If all goes well, you then evolve to station three, true love, when the infatuation of fusion is transmuted into the ecstasy of union. But the initial infatuation with another is one of the places, long after infancy, in which the pre-personal reappears in our lives.[1]

Station 2: Separate Self: Level One Personal

In this station you move from the pre-personal to the first personal stage of human development. This is when the personality, sometimes referred to as the ego, or separate self, comes online. The formation of personality and ego is a wonderfully healthy and necessary stage. You learn to experience yourself as a separate entity among many other separate entities, with your own boundaries and identity. The separate self is born. You feel joy at your success and frustration at your failure. At this station, the distinction between your false self, True Self, and Unique Self does not yet appear.

In this station you are wonderfully caught up in the glory of your story. In the best expression of this station, you are not thinking about your story; you are simply living it. There is great potential depth at this level of consciousness, expressed in part by a direct and unflinching recognition of what is. There comes a time when, in order to grow, you need to get over the fantasy of your idealized life and start recognizing the story of your life for what it is. You embrace your life in all of its complexity, ecstasy, and pain. You can bear it all, and you delight in it all, because it is your life. And in claiming your life as it is, you start to feel something deeply right about it and about yourself. There emerges in you a willingness to take absolute responsibility for everything that happens in your life. You are fully identified with your story. You are a player in your life and not a victim of its circumstances.

Many teachers like to say, "You are not your story." They are right, but only partially. They fail to distinguish between the ego story and the Unique Self story. But there is also great wisdom in this first level of the personal, the station of ego and personality. The ego *prefigures* the Unique Self. And as we shall see, there are many important stations through which you must still evolve toward your full depth and enlightenment. In the next stages of development, you will need to first clarify your story and then to dis-identify with it, in order to return to your ego story at a much higher level of consciousness, the level of Unique Self. While first glimmerings of Unique Self appear at this level of separate self, it can only fully be realized when ego gets over itself.

Station 3: False Self

False self is the unhealthy form of separate self. In this station, you take an essential step in the transformation and evolution of your identity. It is here that you begin to consciously deploy what Freud called the observing ego. Your ability to see the inner structure of your personality comes online. As you separate and look at the story of your life as an object, its contours and patterns begin to become clear to you. You begin to recognize some of the core beliefs that have defined and sometimes deformed your life. Certain core mind-sets start to stand out. You see that you have a particular way of fixing your attention, of stabilizing yourself with familiar and deeply held beliefs.

Just as we get settled in the story of who we are, something amazing, something startling happens. We see that we have been telling a story. The entire narrative that we have formulated, the one that we have become so accustomed to, so comfortable with, slips from our subjective experience and becomes an object, an artifact. In Robert Kegan's insight, the subject of one level of development becomes the object of the next level of development. In this station, the essential practice is that of "making subject object." The understanding of this stage of the journey is based in part on the pioneering work of the great psychologists Robert Assagioli, Oscar Ichazo, and others, which reveals how the fixation of attention, which creates a false sense of self, is the very mechanism that prevents us from uncovering our deeper nature. Your fixation is the particular prism through which you see the world, the way in which, very early in your life, your attention fixated into a particular pattern. This fixation of attention into a particular slant of seeing will naturally produce a distorted picture of your identity, which is your false self. Your false self is the unhealthy and distorted expression of your separate self.

Your false self-fixation often expresses itself in a sentence or series of sentences: "I am not safe." "I am not enough." "I am bad." "I am too much." You live inside your sentence. You need to step outside of your sentence in order to genuinely realize your True Self.

Recognizing these patterns, transcending them, and deploying them skillfully are the next critical steps in your evolution. To walk toward your enlightenment, you must recognize your fixations, break their hold on you, and cleanse the doors of your perception.

To recognize your false self, you must first see it. This is the process of making subject—your false self—into object; your false self becomes an object that you can see and therefore change.

The discernment of the observing ego allows you to take the first steps out of your false self into your real life. You still identify with your separate self, but without the distorting smoke and mirrors of your false self.

Station 4: True Self—Classical Enlightenment: Impersonal

In this station we make the momentous, freeing leap from the personal to the transpersonal. This has been called by some, the liberation from the personal, and the great realization of the impersonal. It would be more accurate to say that it is liberation from the ego personality, which is only level-one of the personal. This level of the personal is transcended only to reappear in clarified form at the level of Unique Self, but first we must realize our True Selves.

We are ready and even yearning to evolve beyond our separate-self ego. We are no longer able to adhere to an identification with self that is painfully limited. The space beyond the story, the awareness beyond the fixations of attention, and the contracted conception of self now become the foreground instead of the background. This is the classical stage of ego dissolution. You realize your True Nature. Your identity shifts from your separate-self ego to your True Self. You move to transcend your personality and identify with your essence. This is the change that changes everything.

Sometimes this dissolution occurs spontaneously, sometimes through overwhelming pain or extreme fatigue; at other times, it emerges as the fruition of years of dedicated study and practice. Yet even at this stage of development, the ego does not disappear. Rather the ego is freed from its own narcissism and becomes an ally. You never evolve beyond ego. You evolve beyond your exclusive identification with ego.

As you begin to dislodge from your exclusive identification with the separate self, as you become disillusioned, you may be fearful or anxious, longing for the old, solid ground of your narrow identity. At the same time, your growing sense is that you are part of an infinitely larger context. Understand that this is not a one-time event, but a continuous process of death and rebirth at each and every moment.

At this station, you engage in spiritual practice in order to dislodge your identity from the hell of separation, and you begin to realize your identity as the eternal Witness, as Big Mind/Big Heart, as the effortless spacious awareness behind this moment and every moment. You recognize your profound interconnectedness with others and the world. You realize that you are part of the larger field of love, intelligence, and creativity underlying All-That-Is. You reach beyond time and taste eternity, stepping out of the stream of past, present, and future, consenting to the full presence of the unchanging Now.

Station 5: Unique Self—The New Enlightenment: Level Two Personal

At the fifth station you witness the emergence of Unique Self. The personal comes back online at a higher level of consciousness. You realize that your True Self is not merely an indistinct part of a larger unification, but expresses itself uniquely, and that you have a unique role to play in the evolutionary unfolding. The personal face of your True Self is your Unique Self. You are able to consciously incarnate the evolutionary impulse toward healing and transformation that initiates, animates, and guides reality. No one else in the world can respond as you can to the unique need of *All-That-Is*, that is yours and only yours to address, and the place of your full liberation and power.

Awakening to your Unique Self has been called the "Pearl beyond Price" by the Sufi adherents, or *"ani* after *ayin"* by Kabbalists. It is alluded to as "Cosmic Consciousness assuming individual form" in the *Yoga Vasistha* of Hinduism.

Unique Self is not just another subtle disguise of the ego. Not in the least. Unique Self is rather the personal face of True Self. Unique Self is the antidote to the grasping of ego. In one moment you are fully alive, dynamically reaching for love and manifestation, and yet you are willing to let go of any attachment in the next moment. Your ego is still present, but you have moved beyond exclusive identification with your ego. Your

Unique Self, which begins to reveal itself at the level of personality, comes to full flower only after freeing itself from the grasping of ego through genuine and repeated experiences of ego clarification and transcending. Unique Self also shows up fleetingly in peak experiences in conjunction with parallel appearances of True Self. An example of this might be a moment of "flow" sometimes called "being in the zone," when ego temporarily drops, and a felt or even lived experience of Unique Self becomes temporarily available.

This stage is hinted at in the Tenth Ox herding picture in Buddhism, one of ten snapshots of enlightenment. In the tenth picture, the man walks back to the marketplace—and I would add, in order to offer his Unique Gifts and to perform the unique *bodhisattva* obligations that can and must be fulfilled by him alone.

Evolutionary Unique Self

It is not enough, however, to awaken only to your unique expression of True Self. There is a second critical dimension of awakening that is essential to Unique Self-realization. I received a direct transmission of this second dimension of Unique Self enlightenment from my lineage teachers who are best described as evolutionary mystics.

Isaac Luria, the teacher of my teachers, the great evolutionary mystic of the Renaissance period, taught that every action that a person takes must be with the explicit consciousness and intention of *Tikkun. Tikkun* is best translated as the evolutionary healing and transformation of all of reality. Every action must be invested with evolutionary intention. In Luria's language it must be *leshem yichud*, meaning for the sake of the evolutionary integration and transformation of all of reality.

To the evolutionary mystics, to awaken means not necessarily to have a profound mystical state experience in which you feel all of being living in you; rather, to awaken is to dramatically, yet simply, shift your alignment. To no longer align with your will, but with God's will.

To awaken to your Unique Self means to awaken to the impulse to evolve, which is the divine creativity surging in you at this very moment, reaching toward the good, the true, and the beautiful. To awaken to your Unique Self is to realize—as the evolutionary mystics taught us—that you live in an evolutionary context. As my teacher Abraham Kook writes, "all of reality"—matter, body, mind, soul, and spirit—"is always evolving." To be a mystic is to know something of the interior face of the cosmos. The novice knows today what only the most advanced souls knew five hundred years ago, that evolution is the inner mechanism of mystery.

Station 6: Unique Shadow

In the post-enlightenment experience, there are still layers to be shed. Even when we are most expansive, most identified with All-That-Is, small pockets of identity are kept out of our awareness, although they are experienced quite directly by everyone around us. You simply can't see them directly, even though recognizing them would free up your energy and directly facilitate a more powerful and beautiful expression of your Uniqueness. This is what is called, both in some of the great traditions and in modern psychology, your shadow.[2]

Learning to recognize and do shadow work is one of the challenges of the full journey of Unique Self. Although shadow work begins at the level of separate self, the full completion of your shadow work is directly connected to your realization of Unique Self. The common understanding of shadow is the negative material about your self that you are unable to own in your first person. This negative material—your jealousy, pettiness, fear, rage, brutality—is understood to be generic. The same core material is said to show up and be repressed into shadow, to a greater and larger degree, by everyone. This is a true but highly partial understanding of shadow.

In Unique Self teaching, we evolve the shadow work conversation and realize that shadow is not generic—shadow is intensely personal. This is a critical evolutionary unfolding of our understanding of shadow.

Your personal shadow is your Unique Shadow. Your Unique Shadow is your disowned Unique Self, the unavoidable result of a life yet unlived. Shadow is not merely your repressed negative material. Shadow is your disowned, denied, or distorted Unique Self. Your Unique Self and your Unique Shadow are a double helix of light and dark coiled into the patterns of becoming.

Remember William Blake's teaching on wisdom and folly: "if the fool would follow his folly, he would become wise."[3] In precisely the same way, you can follow the path of your Unique Shadow back to your Unique Self.

Station 7: Your Unique Gift

The obligation that wells up from your evolutionary realization of Unique Self is your responsibility to give the gifts that are yours alone to give, gifts that are desired and needed by the rest of creation. Every human being has a particular set of gifts to offer in the world. Your Unique Perspective gives birth to what I call your Unique Gift.

The ability to offer this gift freely and fully depends on your ability to free yourself of limiting and false notions of who you are, and to instead identify with your larger service. And beautifully, when this happens you are also able to allow others to be fully who they are as Unique Beings: complete, whole, and specific. This is one of the litmus tests of whether you are in Unique Self or in ego, whether you are able to joyously recognize and affirm the Unique Self of others without feeling that they are taking something that is yours.

Your Unique Gift is the particular contribution that you can make to the evolution of consciousness, which can be made by no one else who ever was, is, or will be. Both the overwhelming desire and ability to give your Unique Gift is a direct and spontaneous expression of your Unique Self-realization. Your Unique Gift, whether public or private, is your divine evolutionary gift to All-That-Is. It is the very face of God, the unique face of evolution alive and awake, in you, as you, and through you.

Some of our gifts are modest, private, and intimate; some are larger than life and have dramatic impact in the public sphere. Some of our gifts are actively given; others emerge from the very uniqueness of our being and presence.

This last point is subtle but essential. Unique Self contains in it something of the old idea of "answering the call" that is essential in Kabbalah and Protestant theology. But it is much more than that. Your Unique Self expresses itself in your Unique Being as well as in your Unique Becoming. Unique Self might have a public face, but it can also be utterly private. A hermit may live Unique Self no less than the President of the United States.

Station 8: Unique Vow, Unique Obligation

In the Buddhist tradition, the *bodhisattva* is one who seeks Buddhahood through practicing noble action. The *bodhisattva* vows to postpone his or her complete awakening and fulfillment until all other beings are awakened and fulfilled.[4] In Kabbalah this same archetype is called the *Tzadik*. The determining factor in their actions is compassion, deployed by utilizing the highest insight and wisdom. The realization of Unique Self may be regarded as *bodhisattva* activity, the unique manifestation of wisdom and guidance. The Unique Self *bodhisattva* vow is an expression of evolutionary joy and responsibility, even as it is a commitment to the fulfillment of your evolutionary obligation.

Many of us recoil when we hear the word "obligation." We identify obligation with arbitrarily imposed limitations set by the church or state that suffocate the naturally free human being. Let's inquire for a moment what obligation might mean at a higher level of consciousness, rather than the obligation imposed by an authority external to you. This inquiry yields the deeper truth that obligation is the ultimate liberation. Obligation frees you from ambivalence and allows you to commit 100 percent to the inherent invitation that is the unique obligation present in every unique situation.

Obligation at this level of consciousness is created by the direct and clear recognition of authentic need that can be uniquely addressed by you and you alone. For example, let's say you are stuck on a lush tropical island with another person. There is abundant food. The problem is, due to a physical ailment, this person is unable to feed herself. Are you obligated to feed her? Most people would agree that in this situation, you have an absolute obligation to feed her. Why is this so? It is based on what I call the fivefold principle of authentic obligation.

First, there is a need.
Second, it is a genuine and not a contrived need.
Third, you clearly recognize the need.
Fourth, you are capable of fulfilling the need.
Fifth, the need can be uniquely addressed by you and you alone.

The combination of these five factors creates your Unique Obligation to give the Unique Gift that can be given only by you in this moment. We commonly understand obligation to be the opposite of love. In the original Hebrew, however, love and obligation are the same word. Authentic obligation is a natural by-product of authentic love.

To live your Unique Self and offer your Unique Gift is to align yourself with the evolutionary impulse and fulfill your evolutionary obligation. The realization of your Unique Self awakens you to the truth that there is a Unique Gift that your singular being and becoming offers the world, which is desperately needed by All-That-Is, and can be given by you and you alone. There is no more powerful and joyous realization available to a human being. It is the matrix of meaning that fills your life and is the core of your Unique Self Enlightenment.

CHAPTER FIVE

THE STORY OF STORY
ONLY HALF THE STORY

TEACHERS OF ENLIGHTENMENT have told you that you must give up your story to be free, that you must leave behind your personal history to be liberated. Story limits you to your skin-encapsulated ego.

This is a deep and true teaching. But it is only half the truth.

Classical Western psychology has told you that the road to health requires you to focus on the drama of your personal story. It has created a container called therapy—which is exclusively focused on your story.

This is a deep and true teaching. But it is only half the truth.

Here is the other half of the story. There is a story you need to leave behind to achieve liberation. However, there is also a story you must radically embrace and live, and without which you can never realize your enlightenment.

The History of Story

Prehistoric humans, embedded in nature, understanding neither the full dignity nor the full terror of their separate self, told only primitive stories. This is because they did not yet need the artifice of narrative to cover up their terror. Death terror is born from a larger sense of time, which emerged together with the experience of being a separate self—apart and against nature. The development of farming created the ability to store food for tomorrow, because the hunger and challenge of today had been met. This was a novel evolutionary emergence that was substantively different from the experience of the hunter-gatherers, who were embedded in the cycles of nature, almost completely absorbed in warding off the threats that faced them *today*. With separate self and an expanded sense of time, a new form of anxiety and terror was born; at the same time, the stories of culture were born to cover up the fear.

There is, however, a second reason why story is directly related to the emergence of the self. This second reason is absolutely essential to understand for your enlightenment.

With the emergence of self, the full dignity of the individual slowly began to dawn on humans. Human beings joyfully realized that they had infinite value, adequacy, and dignity, that they are an end unto themselves. There was a new knowing that personal story matters.

The ego was born out of this movement into individuation. Emerging out of the pre-personal subconscious, the ego was the assertion of the dignity of the personal (personal = personal story). With the emergence of self came the first glimmering recognition of uniqueness. Remember: the separate self prefigures the Unique Self. As Kashmir Shaivism teacher Sally Kempton pointed out to me, in the Hindu tantric tradition, the same Sanskrit word—*Aham*—is used to designate both the individual-ego self and spirit in the first person, the One Self whose I-ness encompasses All-That-Is. The same is true, as we have already pointed out, in the original Hebrew: I (*ani*)-no-thing (*ayin*)-I (*ani*). In tantric philosophical texts, the great I, or pure, absolute awareness, is called *Purno-aham Vimarsha*, the "full or complete I-experience." These are early glimmerings of the Unique Self teaching in which the ego prefigures Unique Self. The great lie of ego, which must be dismantled, is its belief in a separate, isolated self, disconnected and alienated from the larger whole of other, God, and ground.

When we talk of the ultimate dignity of the story, we refer not to the egoic story of the separate self, but rather to the magnificent, courageous, and poignant love story of the Unique Self.

The violation of human dignity through slavery, violence, bearing false witness, or any other form of subtle or brutal manipulation is a violation of story and hence a defacing of God.

"Form" is another word for story. To paraphrase the Heart Sutra, there is no awareness without story and no story without awareness. Form and emptiness, story and nonstory, are one. When we say that God is one or that reality is nondual, we mean that form and awareness, story and nonstory, are but different expressions of the One.

Expand Your Story

I have referred before in this book to a painful period in my life during which my world as I knew it came crashing down. Had I only tried to understand what had happened within the narrow framework of my individual life with its personal betrayals and tragedy, I would have had no hope of emerging from the story. It was only by expanding my personal story to its mythic dimensions that I was able to emerge not only unbroken, but paradoxically gifted a kind of love and wholeness that was previously only available to me in ecstatic states. It was only the larger mythic understanding that allowed me to hold the betrayal and searing pain in the larger context of love and transformation.

I called my dear friend Jean Houston several weeks after the tragedy. We had just met at a wonderful public dialogue that we had done together in front of a large audience in Ashland, Oregon. Jean's advice to me was unambiguous and direct: "mythologize, don't pathologize." She asked me, "What is the greater myth that calls you to a new and deeper destiny that was not available to you before?"

And then without waiting for my response, she answered her own question. "Marc," she said, "you would have never left Israel and never stopped teaching primarily in your narrow Jewish context. God needed you teaching on the world stage. You were unavailable. You received many hints, but you did not listen, lost as you were in your laudable loyalty to your people and tradition. So God arranged a trial by fire that would exile you—perhaps forever—from all you called home. This trial of exile and humiliation is your hero's journey, your mythic tale meant to purify you so that you will be able to meet the next call of your destiny."

In that moment, Jean's larger, mythic story utterly shifted my perspective on everything that had happened. It took several years and a few other attempts to leave the world stage and find my way back to what I thought was my obligation and my home, until I finally surrendered to Jean's grand mythic reading. At that point, somehow—almost in a manner that was beyond my control—I coined the term "World Spirituality." And now I find myself midwifing (with Ken Wilber and other cultural leaders) an international movement in consciousness, aimed at articulating and enacting an evolutionary World Spirituality that has the depth and power to meet the immense and unique global challenges of our time.

Sometimes in the wake of a crisis your story seems to crash to a sudden ending, and all meaning seems to evaporate. You break down. Tragedy and disaster, in small or large portions, can undermine the narrative coherence of your life. You lose the thread of your story. When you lose the thread of the story and get lost in your loneliness, you sometimes go to therapists to regain your way. Your therapist may at times have a vital role to play in helping you find your way in your small story. But all too often, your story is diminished in the process.

Psychology, suggests contemporary philosopher Ernest Becker, tends to reduce human experience. It can disenchant human beings, estranging them from a sense of ultimate value. You want to focus your love on the absolute measure of power and value, and the therapist tells you that your urge is based upon your early conditioning and is therefore relative. You want to find and experience the marvelous, and the therapist tells you how matter-of-fact everything is, how clinically explainable are all of your deepest motives and guilt. You are thereby deprived of the absolute mystery your Unique Self requires. The only omnipotent power that remains is the psychologist who explained it away. And so patients cling to the analyst with all of their might, and dread the termination of therapy.

Psychological myth tends to reduce your deepest yearnings and needs to a set of uninspiring, pitiful human drives that are beyond your control and ignoble at their core. Unique Self-consciousness tells you that while the human condition might at times be tragic, it is never pitiful, and it is always full of hope.

The Grace of the Story

If you can continue to remember to value story, the grace of the story will rise again. The story will gift you with a deeper narrative, and you will begin to see the patterns that connect. The great story takes you out of the narrow pettiness of tired details and into the rich texture of the wider evolutionary context. This is precisely what happened to me and what can happen to you if you but revision your story in the heroic and mythic terms that address the deepest longing of your unfinished dream.

Larger patterns of meaning emerge. You need to call forth the wonder of your story. When you call forth the wonder of your story, you align yourself with the evolutionary impulse that loves you so much that it personalized itself as you. That is what the Unique Self mystics mean when they say that God loves stories. Great story is like a force field, clearing away the many unrelated and seemingly minor plots of your life with overarching meaning and significance.

The Loss of Memory

We all are inheritors of memories and stories larger than our individual lives. You carry the collective experiences that make you old and wise beyond your age or your local knowing.

You are a deeper well than your life history allows. The local stories of your life are entwined in the larger evolutionary story breaking out the world over. And so you must also tell mythic stories. Myth holds a memory larger than your individual story. That is why passionate engagement in a religion or spiritual tradition is so vital to the impoverished modern soul. Joseph Campbell is reported to have said, "A myth is something that never was, but is always happening." It is for this precise reason that myth allows you to regain access to the deep coding's of source that live in your story. Myth breaks your self-contraction.

Not all myths are the same. Some are rooted in lower consciousness, others in higher consciousness. An egocentric myth is not the same as a worldcentric myth. A racist myth does not express truth in the same way as an evolutionary myth. You must deploy the necessary discernment. The miracle of the story is that it allows a different interpretation at every level of consciousness.

But without myths, without the larger stories, you remain stuck in the self-absorption of your narcissistic ego.

Myths demand that you mythologize. When you mythologize, you are freed from the obsessive need to pathologies, demonize, or anesthetize. A big failure takes on a different perspective when you mythologize it. Recognize that failure is part of the hero's journey; transform it into a space of insight that catalyzes your next, greater evolutionary leap. That which seemed like a tragic detour of fate is revealed to be a fractal wave of your destiny and destination. When you mythologize, you regain voice. With your reclaimed voice, you may once again read aloud what my friend Jean Houston has called the unread vision of your higher dream.[1]

The Great Story of Evolution and the Democratization of Enlightenment

We live in the time of the annunciation of a new myth, the great story of evolution. In the language of Unique Self mystic Abraham Kook, this myth raises "the public center of gravity to moral heights and ecstatic joy" in a way that was virtually unattainable in previous eras. Kook and De Chardin, inspired by evolutionary philosophers like Sri Aurobindo and Luria, embrace evolution as the highest and most noble expression of the ethical meaning of our lives on Earth.

Kook writes, "The deep understanding of the evolutionary context in forming our vision of the future exalts man to a moral pinnacle of spirit, radically raising the bar of his ethical responsibility."[2]

Aligning with the evolutionary impulse and taking responsibility for the entire process was, for the last several hundred years, limited to a very small circle of elite mystics. They functioned as an *axis mundi*. (Axis mundi, literally "cosmic axis," is an essential proto-evolutionary teaching that lives in all the great traditions.) It was their task to steady the world with the unbroken clarity and purity of their intention. The World Tree, the Pole in Sufism, the world mountain (*Meru*) in Hinduism, the pillar of light in Mayan and Kabbalistic lore, the rod connecting Heaven and Earth, Jacob's Ladder—these are different names for the *axis mundi*. The cosmic axis, according to the perennial wisdom traditions, incarnates in a human being, who is a vital point of connection embracing Heaven and Earth. The *Tzadik Hador*, the thirty-six just men upon whom the world rests, and the *Jagadguru* or "world teacher" are names for this figure or group of figures. It is to this that Jesus referred when he said, "I am the light," and when he said, "I and my father are one. When you see me, you see the one who sent me."

Not All Stories Are Equal

We all have a thousand covers that allow us to close our hearts. To stay open as love is the invitation of your life. You cannot do so, however, by abandoning the integrity of the story. Your ego becomes so obsessed with your hurt or fear that you are sometimes seduced to close your heart, rather than do the work of story. Hearing your enemy's story—really hearing—may be just what is needed to make them no longer your enemy.

Yet it is also true that not all myths are the same. Not all stories have equal gravitas. You may hear your enemy's story, and they may remain your enemy. Not all interpretations of *Romeo and Juliet* have equal value. There are some readings of this play that so egregiously violate the sense and facts of the story that they are simply wrong. There is a hierarchy of stories. Some stories are more true than others. False hierarchies most often manifest as what we refer to as dominator hierarchies. They are built by assigning to something or someone a value that it does not have—for example, "White people are more evolved than black people" is a false hierarchy. Or, "People born in Tibet are superior to people born in Kansas." These are false hierarchies, false stories, and false myths. The truest story is able to take in the greatest number of perspectives and align them with the greatest number of facts in all the quadrants of reality, in the best way possible.

The simplest example is in the realm of justice. A judge must first hear both sides of the story. The judge must examine the hurt that is claimed. Is it true? What are the potential hidden motives of everyone concerned? What are the consequences of each possible course of action? At that point, the judge must sit carefully for some period of time to allow the fullness of the facts and perspectives from all sides to emerge.

When we speak of a judge, we do not refer to the formal position of the judicial officer in the court. Rather, by "judge" we mean anyone whose decision has power over the fate of another's life. The more power, the more responsibility and therefore the more care and love required. The judge must be a lover. Judgment is a process of radical love. And love is a perception.

The art of the lover is the perception of the True Nature, the Unique Self, of every moment, person, and situation in the larger context of All-That-Is. Only a Unique Self can judge fairly with love. If you are not in your Unique Self, then you need something from the judgment. You are partial, meaning you are locked in your part nature, disconnected from your larger self. Your small self is grasping to steal from the judgment what it can, for its own survival.

Your True Self plus your clarified personal perspective, which is your Unique Self, is the only possible source of right judgment. You may go through the entire love process of judgment—hearing and evaluating all motives and stories—and someone may still remain an enemy. You may decide, as the Dalai Lama once said to me, that we need to "deploy violence against the enemy when there is no other choice. Even so, we never stop loving them." Do what you need to do, but never put the enemy out of your heart. Forgiveness and reconciliation will then remain an ever-present possibility.

CHAPTER SIX

EGO AND UNIQUE SELF

ONE OF THE MOST IMPORTANT DISTINCIONS that we have pointed out is the difference between ego and Unique Self. As I've stated, they represent two very different levels of consciousness. At the level of ego, you must let go of the illusion of specialness. At the level of Unique Self, you must embrace the infinite gorgeousness of your specialness, and the obligation that it creates for you to give your deepest unique gifts to the world. Unique Self, which is your Unique Perspective, creates your unique gifts, which in turn creates your unique obligation to offer your gift.

This entire linked set of unfolding realizations is predicated on the discernment between Unique Self and ego. This discernment is essential to prevent ego from hijacking Unique Self. So what we need to do at this point is deepen our grasp of that discernment, which is all-important for the realization of your Unique Self Enlightenment.

Twenty-Five Distincions between Ego and Unique Self

To live a successful life of realization, power, and genuine attainment, you must be able to discern between expressions of your separate self or ego and your Unique Self. In the following section I will draw a number of distinctions between Unique Self and ego. The purpose of these distinctions is to serve as pointing-out instructions that will help you make the discernment between ego and Unique Self in your own first-person experience. The ego and Unique Self dualities that I offer below are—like all dualities—not ultimate.

1) Special or Not Special

Your ego thinks that you are special because you are better or worse than other people. Your Unique Self knows you are special because you are yourself. For the ego, "special" means "better than." For your Unique Self, "special" or "different" means distinct and free from any comparison or point of reference. Your specialness is your spontaneous experience of your essence.

2) Action or Reaction

Ego reacts. Unique Self acts. Your ego is constantly in reaction to outside stimuli. It never thinks a spontaneous thought. It rarely acts because it is moved to do so by a freely arising thought or desire.

Unique Self is moved to action by the power and joy of its own authentic original impulse.

3) Imitation or Originality

Ego imitates. Unique Self is original. Your ego is trapped in imitation. For the ego is, by its very definition, in limitation. Limitation leads to imitation. So the ego is always living the life of limitation based on imitation, which leads to mindless competition. Your ego is in constant competition, which leads to compulsive comparison and dissatisfaction. Originality, which is a quality of Unique Self, freed from the tyranny of comparison, is by its nature both urgently creative and self-satisfied.

Your ego never thinks an original thought. Originality emerges from your Unique Face, which is evoked by contact with your Original Face. "Original face" is the Buddhist way of describing the experience of sustained contact with the eternal, transcendent Ground of Being. Originality gives ego and Unique Self birth to action beyond reaction. Your Unique Becoming emerges from your immersion in Being.

4) Satisfaction or Greed

Your separate self is driven by greed. Greed is not the want of anything specific. Rather, it is insatiable want that creates perpetual anxiety. Insatiable want is a structure of the egoic mind, which seeks more and more identity enhancers to confirm its existence. Satisfaction and ego are opposites.

Give the ego everything, and it will not be satisfied. Give the Unique Self anything, and it will be grateful and satisfied. Satisfied, not resigned. Satisfaction emerges from the fullness of whatever the moment brings.

Satisfaction comes from contact with Being and from doing your radical, intense best in the world of Becoming without attachment to outcome. Being is all one, so any moment of Authentic Being gives infinite satisfaction. Becoming is an expression of the evolutionary impulse and not merely of the egoic drive to achieve. So for Unique Self, your very best is always good enough. For your ego, your very best is never good enough. This is why the ego is the source of all your suffering. It always wants more to fill its greed.

5) Enough or More

Your ego thinks that there is never enough to go around. It always needs more to feel like it exists at all. Your Unique Self knows that it is enough. Your Unique Self knows that there is enough to go around. Your Unique Self strives for more, not to fill the emptiness but as an expression of the fullness of its being—bursting forth as the evolutionary impulse of the cosmos.

6) Ego Story or Unique Self Story

Enlightenment requires your ability to discern between your ego story and your Unique Self story. Your separate-self egoic personality has needs. It wants to make itself feel secure. So your ego tells you a story about yourself that makes you feel safe, valuable, and worthy. The inability to feel safe, valuable, and worthy is a devastating experience for the ego, one it will ward off at virtually all costs. So the ego hijacks everything that happens to you, and everything that you do, into a story about its own goodness, value, and worth. The ego has a simple if ingenious mechanism for doing this. It disguises its ambition, its drive for power, or its insecure grasping, and converts them into narrative material that supports its own positive self-image. This is how the separate-self ego story develops. It is this story that teachers of True Self correctly tell you to leave behind when they say, "to be enlightened you must let go of your story."

This is an essential part of the process of enlightenment or awakening. What you are essentially doing is dis-identifying with your story or perspective, and then taking a perspective on your perspective.[1] You are letting your story become an object, so that you can see it and understand the root motivations and dynamics that are really at play in your story. When that happens, there is space for your more authentic story to arise, which reflects not the grasping of the separate-self ego but the utterly resplendent uniqueness of your Unique Self. This is your Unique Self Story.

7) Joy or Fear

The Unique Self is in joy. Joy is the natural by-product of living your Unique Self story. The ego is rarely happy and often plagued by an underlying feeling of fear, deadness, or depression. The happiness that the ego does experience is of a heavier and less richly textured quality than the joy of the Unique Self. The joy of the Unique Self is lighter and freer, often verging on the ecstatic.

8) Open Heart or Closed Heart

When the ego's heart breaks, then the heart closes and contracts. When the Unique Self's heart breaks, the heart opens through the pain into greater love. For your ego, the interior face of the cosmos is at best a concept. For Unique Self, the interior face of the cosmos is the infinity of intimacy.

9) Eros or Grasping

The ego is not erotic. Unique Self lives in Eros. To live in Eros means to live with fullness of presence and with a felt sense of wholeness. It is to yearn urgently and ecstatically, without grasping and to experience interiority, the feeling of being on the inside. This is the experience of Unique Self. The ego lives with the feeling of always being on the outside. It fragments, grasps, and never shows up fully present to other. Unique Self lives in Eros.

10) Authentic Freedom or Pseudofreedom

Your ego is a slave that wants to be free. Freedom is the quality that we call autonomy. Your ego, however, understands and experiences freedom/autonomy as freedom from external influence. Only then does ego feel free to do what it wants. Unique Self is free. Unique Self understands and experiences freedom as the freedom to live your Uniqueness and give your deepest gifts in the world.

When you feel yourself demanding your egoic freedom, stop for a moment and feel into it. Do not cover over the emptiness that lies at the root of your desire for freedom and autonomy. Feel into the emptiness. Feel into the hole.

For example: perhaps you are in a relationship that you want to leave. You are chafing to get out of the relationship. But as you contemplate this, stay in the discomfort that you can palpably feel—which lies at the root of this desire. For now, do not give the feeling words. Instead feel the quality of the vacuity and emptiness that arouses the desire.

If you stay in it long enough, the emptiness will begin to fill up with being and presence, with your Unique Being and presence.

What happened?

You have discovered that the root of your desire to be free from another was your disconnection from your own personal essence, your Unique Self. When your Unique Self filled the hole, the desperate desire you felt to leave the group—or the marriage or the job—faded away. That does not mean that you should necessarily stay in the marriage or the job. It does however mean that you will make the decision from a grounded place of full presence as your Unique Self, and are therefore far more likely to make the right decision.

11) King or Servant

Ego is the servant pretending to be a king. You are avoiding stepping into your Unique Self for fear of being a king. Your ego thinks it is God but does not really believe it, so your ego insanely tries to make itself the God it knows it is not. Your Unique Self knows it is God, so it acts in the world with majesty, audacity, and grace.

12) Victim or Player

In your ego, you cling to every petty detail of your story. You never let go of any of your wounds. Your mantra is "I hurt, therefore I am." Therefore, your ego can never wholeheartedly forgive. If it does, the ego's forgiveness is a tactic, not a sacrament. Your Unique Self forgives freely without giving up your own truth.

Your Unique Self is not a victim. It is an audacious player in the Great Story of the evolution of consciousness. This larger perspective allows you to begin to let go of the story of your wounds. As it is replaced by the greater story of your Unique Self, delight and obligation begin to emerge.

13) Betrayal or Loyalty

The ego betrays. The Unique Self is loyal. When you are in your ego, and things go bad, you are willing—in your fear—to betray virtually anyone. Your ego is easily identifiable by the shallowness of its integrity. If you live in Unique Self and things go bad, you find your way, through thick or thin, to a deeper center of spirit.

14) Authentic Friendship or Pseudofriendship

When you are in ego, you might help friends who are successful and even friends who are down, as long as it does not threaten your position. But you are not capable of truly delighting in your deepest heart in a friend's large success. When you are in Unique Self, your deepest heart delights in your friend's success, even if there is nothing in it for you at all.

15) Bigger or Smaller

When you are in ego, people feel smaller when you walk into the room. They feel invisible before you. The result is that they feel depleted and in danger. When you are in your Unique Self, people feel bigger when you walk into the room. They feel seen by you. They feel your desire to love and give to them.

16) Yes or No

Your ego is always contracting and saying, "No." Even when your ego says, "Yes," it is only because it is afraid to say, "No." Your Unique Self is always expanding and saying, "Yes." Even when you say, "No," it is only to make room for a more authentic "Yes."

17) Justice or Injustice

The ego is angry at what is done to it. It very rarely feels the same outrage at what is done to someone else. The Unique Self is not merely outraged against injustice done to its own person; it is hurt and outraged by any and all injustice. The ego often fights large causes of injustice as a way to bolster its grandiosity. Unique Self fights the battles of injustice in its own backyard, even when there is potential collateral damage to its own power and status.

18) Responsibility or Excuse

The ego very rarely takes substantive responsibility. When the ego attempts to take responsibility, it creates a painful, virtually unbearable contraction in the self. So the ego becomes the master of the excuse. The Unique Self is able to take responsibility spontaneously, lightly, and with full gravitas. The Unique Self holds with equal measure of gravitas and ease its own responsibility and its rightful anger at injustice. Usually, the ego advises the other person to "take responsibility," while the ego itself wallows in the real and imagined offenses that it has suffered.

19) Paradox or Splitting

The ego is always splitting. It always sees dualities, and it cannot hold paradox or complexity. For the ego, others are either enemies or friends. Actions are either good or bad. The separate-self ego has a very hard time stably holding perspectives other than its own for extended periods of time. The Unique Self can naturally hold paradox. Contact with the transcendent within the large field of divine reality allows for the holding of opposites. Sacred outrage and equanimity live in paradoxical harmony within the Unique Self.

20) Past or Present

The ego lives in the past, thinking it is the present. Therefore, the ego unconsciously confuses past with present. The ego is unable to create intimacy, which means meeting each other in the fullness of the present moment. To make real contact, you must be personal and present. Only the Unique Self can make contact. For the Unique Self, the present moment consciously includes the past and anticipates the future.

The Unique Self does not confuse the past with the present. When the past comes up in the present, the Unique Self recognizes it for what it is: the past coming up in the present. The Unique Self then uses the present moment to heal the past. The Unique Self recognizes that the patterns of the past have no true foothold or power in the present.

21) Special Relationship or Open as Love

Your ego always seeks the "special relationship"—in the egoic sense—to cover the pain of emptiness, and thinks the "special relationship" is better than all other relationships. The Unique Self does not limit love to one person, even though the traditional definition of marriage or a committed relationship can limit you to one partner at a time. The Unique Self lives open as love in the world.

22) Love or Fear

The isolated ego is the root cause of murder, war, and virtually all human suffering. The ego feels its own fragility, its limits, and its ultimate powerlessness. As a result, the ego grasps for ways to assert power and experience aliveness. This causes the acting out of all forms of shadow. When the contraction of ego uncoils, your Unique Self experiences all of the good—personal love, responsibility, compassion, ethical action, activism, and all the rest—that you previously thought was accessible only through your assertion of a separate self.

23) Eternity or Death

The ego strives for immortality it can never achieve, and therefore displaces its grasping for eternity onto projects of control and conquest. The Unique Self experiences authentically what the ego longs for mistakenly—namely the recognition that it is divine and therefore eternal.

This distinction is essential and therefore deserves a brief clarification. The separate self emerges at a certain stage of human history and at a certain stage in the development of the individual human being.[2] As the sense of separate self solidifies, so too does the terror of death. The person feels correctly that death is wrong, that they should not have to die. They feel that they are eternal and should live forever. They are right. The core intuition of immortality could not be more correct. But locked as they are in separate-self ego awareness, they misapply that core intuition in two ways.[3]

First, because they are utterly identified with the ego, they apply their intuition of immortality to the egoic separate self. They think that the ego will live forever. Second, because they are identified with the now-eternalized ego, and yet at the same time are gripped by the fear of death, which is oblivion to the ego, they seek all sorts of Viagra-like identity enhancers. They make the finite goods of the world into infinite goods. Money, surplus goods, power, accumulated pleasures—all become identity enhancers for the ego. Their purpose is to give the ego a felt sense of its immortality. But since the ego is not immortal, all of these death-denying immortality projects are doomed to failure.

Even though the ego does make these two essential mistakes, the ego's intuitions are not wrong. When the mistakes are corrected at the level of Unique Self, the truth behind those intuitions can emerge. After you dis-identify with your separate self, your Unique Self appears as a distinct and indivisible part of the Eternal One. It is in your Unique Self that you realize your immortality. The Unique Self expresses correctly the mistakenly applied, but inwardly correct, intuition of the ego.

24) Pleasure: Delusion or Divine

Money, power, and pleasure, when experienced at the level of ego, appear separate from the divine field and trap you in the clutches of grasping and striving. When experienced from the level of enlightened consciousness, money, power, and pleasure are expressions of your Unique Self touching the divine. Pleasure from the place of Unique Self is experienced as a divine caress reminding you that the world is sane and good. Ego pleasures feel narcissistic, and solidify the coiled contraction into small self. They never satisfy; you are constantly driven to get more and more, and someone else's pleasure makes you feel your own lack. The same pleasure experienced from the consciousness of Unique Self expands your heart and consciousness into the love-intelligence, love-beauty, and love-pleasure of All-That-Is. You are satisfied by even the simplest pleasure, and you delight in the pleasure of others.

Similarly, power and money grasped by the ego seek to support the false belief of the separate self that it will live forever. Power and money are used to accumulate goods you do not need, and to acquire superficial control over others in order to assure yourself that you are valuable and worthy. Money and power experienced from the consciousness of Unique Self are gracefully and skillfully deployed with delight for the greater good of all beings.

Separate from the divine field, money, pleasure, and power appear as foolish and even grotesque identity enhancers for the ego. This becomes radically apparent whenever we encounter death. The ego is confused. It fails to discern between separateness and uniqueness, and so the goods of existence are hijacked to serve its own impossible goal of survival—separate from the larger field of love-beauty-pleasure-intelligence from which it was never separate and never can be separated.

Correct intuitions that are hijacked and misapplied by the ego are contextualized and reclaimed at the level of Unique Self. These include eternity and the finite goods of the world, the goodness of pleasure, the divine aspect of power, and more. All of these are reclaimed without grasping at the level of Unique Self.

25) Ego Story or Unique Self Story

Your egoic story can be taken away by the circumstances of life. Your Unique Self story can never be taken away from you. Ego can be taken away from you. Unique Self can never be taken away from you.

Ego Points to Unique Self

Ego is not the villain. Your ego has wisdom to offer you. Ego holds truths that in their clarified form belong to Unique Self. The core truths of Unique Self are distorted by your ego's fear, contraction, and shadow.

What allows qualities that show up in ego to be reclaimed at the level of Unique Self is sustained contact with the transcendent, which shifts your perspective and opens the space beyond fear to do the genuine work of clarification and healing. In this book, I have called contact with the transcendent True Self, the realization of your essential nature.

Ego is pre–True Self.

Unique Self is post–True Self.

Or at least, post some glimmering of True Self, as True Self may show up in a flow experience or in other glimpses of authenticity. After authentic contact with your True Nature—or at least a sustaining glimpse of it—garnered by any of these modalities or others, the gifts of ego can be harvested at the level of Unique Self.

CHAPTER SEVEN

LOVE AND UNIQUE SELF

THE TRUE NATURE OF YOUR VALUES is always revealed in death. At your funeral, you will hear in the eulogies, both in what is spoken and unspoken, something of the essential nature of your life and loyalties. Sometimes, however, before you die, you are strangely privileged with a final invitation to declare where your ultimate loyalty lies. The moments before your death might be joyous or tragic.

It was September 11, 2001. The planes had just crashed into the Twin Towers in Manhattan. People had very short moments to use their cell phones. No one called asking for revenge. No one offered philosophical explanations or profound insights into the nature of reality. People did one thing and one thing only: they called the people close to their heart to say, "I love you." "I love you" is our declaration of faith. Implicit in those words is everything holy.

And yet we no longer really know what we mean when we say, "I love you." It used to mean, "I am committed to you. I will live with you forever." Or it might have meant, "You are the most important person in my life." But it no longer seems to mean that. The old Greek, Thucydides, wrote in his great work *The Peloponnesian War* something like, "When words lose their meaning, culture collapses." When you no longer understand your own deepest declarations of love, you are lost. The very foundation of meaning upon which your world rests is undermined. You lose your way. You become alienated from love, which is your home. Despair, addiction, and numbness become your constant companions. For so many of us, love has lost its luminosity as the organizing principle of our lives. Love seems to have diminished power to locate us and to guide us home. "I love you" has become banal, casual, and desiccated.

One day you feel the love; the next day you do not. One day love holds you in the place of your belonging, and the very next day you are cast out, exiled, and lost. For so many of us, "I love you" has ceased to be a place where we can find our home.

What do you really mean when your highest self says to another, "I love you"? And if I might audaciously add to the question: why do all the great traditions, in one way or another, talk about the obligation to love God and love your neighbor? In the tradition of Kabbalah, this obligation to love God and one another is called a *mitzvah temidit*, a "constant obligation of consciousness." But does this truly resonate with our experience? Actually, if we admit it to ourselves, this injunction makes little sense. How does a human being love God? Is God lovable? Can you touch God, cuddle with God, or actually feel rushing love for God without entering into an altered state?

What emotional affect is there to the love of God? And does not that emotional affect, if it is even an authentic possibility for the common person, seem dangerously close to a kind of blind fundamentalist emotional faith?

How does one love God? And how can one be obligated to love another? How can you obligate an emotion? And can we truly feel love toward all of our neighbors? Isn't love reserved for the very few special people in our lives?

Said differently and more directly, what is love?

To know the way of Unique Self, you must know the way of love.

To find your destination in love, you must consider the reason for all of your detours. You must wonder about all of your wrong turns in love.

Where did you go wrong? Is there something you did not understand about the nature of love?

You are not alone in your questions. There is hardly a person alive who is conscious who has not asked these questions—this writer included. So I will speak to myself through you.

Love Is a Verb

If you are like most highly intelligent and sincere modern seekers, you are making two core mistakes about love. First, you think that love is an emotion. When the emotion is gone, you feel like you are no longer in love and thus can no longer stay in the relationship.

Second, you automatically identify love with a particular emotion. The emotion with which you identify love is usually the emotion of infatuation. Both of these mistaken beliefs are significant obstacles on your path to spiritual liberation. Both of these mistakes obscure love's innate ability to take you home.

Love at its core is not an emotion. Love is a perception. Love is the ultimate verb. Love is a faculty of perception that allows you to see the inner nature of All-That-Is.

To love another human being is to perceive their True Nature. To love is to perceive the infinite specialness and divine beauty of the beloved.

To be a lover is to see beyond the limited and distorting vision of your separate-self contraction.

To be a lover is to see with God's eyes. Your beloved is both your lover and All-That-Is.

To be loved by another human being is to have your True Nature seen. Your True Nature is your Unique Self.

To love God is to let God see with your eyes, to empower God with the vision of your Unique Perspective. You are living out of a passion for God. You are being asked to live with God's eyes.

To act with God's eyes, to react with God's eyes, to write your Book of Life with God's eyes as God would see from your perspective. If you are successful, then your perspective becomes available to God. It finds God and feeds God. It gives God strength and joy. You must consider that being a devotee is nothing but actually being God from a distinct perspective.

To be responsible for this perspective is to declare the truth from this vantage point, but without making it the only perspective, and without any degree of attachment to the vantage point we have clung to from the past—from our previous conditioning. This is what it means to be a lover.

This is the great paradox again and again. To be a lover is to see with God's eyes. To love God is to let God see with your eyes.

Once, I shared this understanding of love with the Dalai Lama. "Beautiful!" he exclaimed with sheer and utter delight.

Beautiful was the Dalai Lama in the direct and delicious expression of his delight. Particularly, he was excited to shift the understanding of love from an emotion to a perception.

It is this precise shift that clears up one of the great mysteries of love. Many great thinkers have been puzzled by the Hebrew wisdom commandment to love. How can you command an emotion? And yet in the evolutionary mysticism of Unique Self teaching, love is the ultimate commandment. Reading the old Hebrew text, "love your neighbor as yourself—I AM GOD," the answer to the puzzle is now clear.

Step one: love is not an emotion. Love is a perception.

"Love your neighbor as yourself " Is the seemingly impossible demand of the Hebrew book of Leviticus, echoed in the New Testament in the book of Matthew. At least this is how the text is usually cited. But the quote, as it is usually cited, is actually missing three words. It's too short. What all too often gets left out of the passage are the three last, and per- haps most crucial, words. The complete verse is, "love your neighbor as yourself—I am God." To love your neighbor is to know that the "I" is God. To love your neighbor is to perceive God's divine beauty in others and let it fill you with wonder and radical amazement. To love your neighbor is to behold with wonder God's infinite specialness. Love is what the Hindus called *Bhakti*, to truly see the other bathed in their own divine radiance.

Love is not an emotion. Love is not infatuation.

Emotions are involuntary reactions that come from the nervous system. The emotion of infatuation is usually a preprogrammed reaction that takes place when you meet someone that you recognize. You recognize them because you remember them. They evoke in you a sense of familiarity and intimacy. They unconsciously remind you of your parents or early caretakers.

The person with whom you are infatuated holds out to you the possibility of completing the unfinished emotional business you have with your mother, father, or early caretakers. Or you fall in love with them as an expression of your unconscious rebellion or alienation from your parents or caretakers, whom you experience as painful or dangerous.

Only when you fall out of infatuation do you see—sometimes for the first time. Before then, your perception is blurred. Infatuation is blind. Love is a magnifying glass. Initially the perception yields a more complex and less rosy picture then the blind adulation of infatuation, but if you stay with it, remain focused, and invest your self with full passion and heart, the perception begins to clarify. You begin to genuinely see the full splendor and beauty of the one you love. The delight of love is a natural result of your perceptions.

Love is perception's gift. Love is a faculty of perception, which allows you to see the inner nature of All-That-Is. Love is a realization. Love is a verb. Love is the true inner nature of All-That-Is. Love is.

Love Is a Perception-Identification Complex

When we say that love is perception, we do not mean it is merely perception. It is, as we have implicitly seen in our discussion till now, a perception-identification complex. And this is not a complex in the Oedipal sense, but rather in the simplest sense of a two-part structure. Love is a two-part formula.

The beloved not only perceives the divine, the Unique Self of her lover; she identifies him with that divinity. She understands his divinity as his essence. She sees and identifies her beloved with his infinite specialness.

This notion of perception identification is most clear in reference to parents and children. You love your kids. The neighbor's kids, however—well, they are just so incredibly rambunctious, annoying, and immature.

In fact, we all recognize that there may be no appreciable difference between your kids and the neighbor's kids. Why then do you love your children and not the neighbor's? Not merely because they're your children, but rather, because they are your children, you are invested in them. This investment causes you to focus your vision on them more intensely than on other kids. The result: you are able to perceive them in ways other people are simply unable to do. You perceive your child's beauty in a way that no one quite grasps.

But perception is not enough. If you are a good parent, you know your child also has faults, and those shortcomings are real. They need to be addressed forthrightly and never swept under the rug. Remember, love is not blind; infatuation is blind. Love is a microscope. Parents should be madly in love with their kids—they should never be infatuated with them.

How is it then that you love your children even after you know their long laundry list of faults? The answer lies in the second step of the love formula, identification. You perceive both your child's goodness and their flaws—but you identify their goodness as the true core of who they are. All the rest you will deal with in whatever way necessary—but you know that the essence of your child is "trailing clouds of glory." And you love them for it. With kids not our own, what we often (wrongly) tend to do is identify the child with their failing or acting out instead of with their infinite specialness and grandeur.

Have any of your friends every gotten engaged, and the response of your circle was something like, "I can't believe it! SHE IS going to marry . . . HIM? Candice . . . is going to marry . . . Tom??!!" We do not understand what she sees in him. But see in him she does. She perceives him, sees him, discloses him in a way that we are unable to access. How did Emily Dickinson say it? "Not 'revelation'—tis—that waits, but our unfurnished eyes." Our eyes are too "furnished" to see the miraculous, infinitely unique gorgeousness that is Tom. To love is to see with unfurnished eyes. But let there be no mistake about it— Tom is stunningly gorgeous. To Candice, the man is a miracle. The word "miracle" comes from the Latin *mirari*, meaning "to behold with rapt attention." Candice has beheld the glory of Tom and found him to be divine. She has seen his infinite uniqueness, the snowflake essence of his soul that most miraculously never melts. To love is to witness the miracle of your beloved. Love is a Unique Self Perception.

Love, Being, and Becoming

To say that love is a perception of the True Nature of things is to recognize that love is subversive. The emperor struts around in his clothes. But he is not really the emperor. He is the servant disguised as the emperor. The separate self in the form of a skin-encapsulated ego rules the roost. The servant has displaced the king. Along comes love, and pierces the heart of all illusions. The true heart opens, and reality reappears in its full and undivided majesty and splendor. The lover is the great hero who ushers in—through the penetrating power of their perception—a new world order.

Sometimes perception is a result of intense and sustained effort. This is called in the old sacred texts "arousal from below." At other times, it is a free gift of the Universe. This is called "arousal from above."

There are moments when your eyes just open with delight. You have been gifted by the Universe with a direct perception of essence. Your heart opens, your breath draws in, and you fall in love for a moment. It might be the ocean, a radiant sunset, the erotic curve of the feminine, or the lean, angular throbbing of the masculine. It might be a thirteen-pedaled rose, a baby, precious stones, or a person fully in their gift.

All of these give you a direct, unearned gift of essence. A gift of love.

The first few examples are images of being. The last example, a person fully in their gift, is an image of manifested becoming. It is the revelation of Unique Self.

The old Hindu Upanishads teach, "Where there is other, there is fear." This describes your consciousness at the level of ego. If, however, you have upleveled your consciousness and are living as Source—from the place of your Unique Self—the teaching changes: "Where there is other, there is love."

The Perception of Love Creates a New Reality

Marriage in the old world served many ends. It created personal security and a stable context for parenting, and it ensured that order, and not chaos, reigned in society. Marriage in the new world is a Unique Self encounter.

As is often the case, an old text contains seeds of the new paradigm. An old Aramaic text reads, "The bride and groom reveal the Shekhinah." What might that mean? Do you know that moment in a wedding when it really happens? It has nothing to do with the music, catering, hall, or any of the other fanfare. It is that fraction of a second when they walk down the aisle or are standing at the altar or under the canopy. You feel the revelation that always waits for our unfurnished eyes. The bride and the groom look at each other. It is a glorious moment of Unique Self perception. They see each other in all of their depth and wonder. At that moment, the marriage is consummated.

But it is even more than that.

We become more—the more we are seen and recognized. The level of love after thirty years of life together is vastly and incomparably deeper than the love available at the wedding altar.

But it is even more than that.

Physics reminds us that perception not only observes but also creates reality. See your beloved at their highest, and you will deepen and empower their highest. You then live with their highest. When you see your beloved at their lowest, you empower and deepen the lowest. You then live with their lowest.

Liquid Love—To See the Future in the Now

Part of perception-identification requires the lover to be a visionary. To touch in the now what might be in the future. The lover's perception intuits unfolding and growth long before it actually manifests. If in any moment you are so enamored that you say, like Goethe's Dr. Faustus, "linger, Thou art fair," you forfeit your soul. For what you have done is to freeze the moment and stop growing. Unique Selves are always unfolding. Unique Self is both a point of origin and a destination. We grow, but we were really always there to begin with—the fully developed lover senses the destination in the point of origin.

The Seer of Lublin, a nineteenth-century biblical mystic, said:

> There are three kinds of friends in the world. An ordinary friend sees you as you appear to be.
> An extra-ordinary friend sees you for what you can be.
> But in the presence of the highest friend—you already are.

To love a person is both to perceive a person and to identify them with the best, not just of who they are, but who they could become. We are not simply human beings; we are human becomings. In fact, in the original Hebrew the words "I am" do not exist. "I am" in Hebrew is rather "I will become." Likewise, in the old Hebrew story, when Moses asks God his name, God answers, *Ekyeh Asher Ekyeh*. Usually this strange and potent phrase is translated as "I am what I am." But the actual translation is "I will be what I will be." God is "will be." God is Becoming.

To love is to see in another what they cannot yet see themselves. "I love them for the person they want to be. I love them for the person they almost are." And somehow, through being loved, we begin to be who we want to be, who we really are. To love is to embrace another, not only as a human being but also as a human becoming.

Words are a freezing of reality. Before I put the chapter down on paper it is infinite, liquid-like, and emerging. The second I pick one of the infinite possible turns of phrase, it becomes frozen. For every word I choose, a thousand others are rejected. How much more of a human violation it is when I freeze another person into what they are at a particular moment. Worse yet to freeze people into their moments of fall and failure. That is a great failure of love.

"Love is a Unique Self Perception" has four words too many. The truth is, quite simply, love is. For love has really been here all the time. Love is the infinite, pulsating erotic energy of life and goodness that is the fabric of Being. When we realize that love is, then we understand ever more deeply that love is but a shift in perception.

The Secret Is in the Eyes

An emotion cannot be commanded; perception can. The emotion of love is neither flickering nor fickle. It is directly dependent on the energy and effort of your perception.

There is an old mystical tradition that the world rests on thirty-six hidden saints. They are the polished gemstones of God's evolutionary creation. Israel, Master of the Good Name, was the leader of this group in his generation. He indulged his disciples with the stories and teachings he would hear from these sacred saints.

"But we want to see them also," begged his students. Day after day they pressed him to reveal the hidden men to them as well.

"So be it," said Israel.

At the close of the following week, he said to his disciples. "So . . . were you not impressed by them greatly?"

"But what do you mean?" replied the astonished disciples, "impressed by who? We didn't see a single saintly soul."

"Ahh," said the master. "So you did not see them. That doesn't mean they were not there. Remember the beggar who came for a loaf of bread? A saint! And the young widow crying that she had lost her husband? She too was one of them. And the juggler in the circus on Thursday? He too was of their number."

"Holy disciples," said the master to his beloved students. "The secret is in the eyes. The secret is in the eyes."

I bless you, dear friend and reader, with eyes to see. To see the saint hidden in each passing face. Who knows, perhaps you too are one of their number, so well hidden that even you have yet to perceive your hidden light.

Self-Love

Israel, Master of the Good Name, has a wonderful teaching on the Hebraic mandate "Love your neighbor as you love yourself." First, it is a statement of fact—you love your neighbor precisely as much as you love yourself. You can only perceive another's greatness if you have glimpsed and believe in your own.

Self-love is self-perception.

If this is so, then a powerful question arises! How do you love your self when you know all of your foibles, pathologies, and blemishes? If self-love is self-perception, does not honest perception yield all the reasons that we are not lovable? And yet most of us manage, at least to some degree, to love ourselves. Is it just self deception? No, not at all. Love, as we have unpacked it together, is not merely perception. It is a perception-identification complex. Self perception means that, although I am aware of the full complexity of my personae—the good, the bad, and the ugly—I identify the essence of who I am with my good. With my good, loving, giving, creative, and generous self.

That does not mean I deny my beast. It is, of course, critical to integrate all of me into my self-picture.

But the essence, the core of who I am, remains my goodness, virtue, and beauty. To love your self is to identify your self as part of the Shekhinah. Writes Master Israel, "To love yourself is to love the Shekhinah." Not to love yourself is to send the Shekhinah into exile. So proclaim the Kabbalists.

To which Rumi adds:

> By God, when you see your beauty
> you will be the idol of yourself.

In your deepest nature you must know that you are the hero of your story. In your deepest nature you are love, grace, strength, and splendor. Now you must decide to identify with your deepest nature. Do you focus on your innocence or your guilt? Do you focus on your inevitably dirty hands, or on your eternally pure spirit? To love yourself or anyone else, you need to know that your innocence is your essence. That your innocence is never lost. That you remain always worthy of love, even as you muster all of your energy and commitment to the evolution of your essence.

Self-love is a shift in perception in which you embrace—maybe for the first time—the full wonder of who and what you are. That is what it means to accept God. Perception always begins with knowledge—self-knowledge. Self-knowledge does not mean long-term intensive psychotherapy that explores every nook and cranny of your psyche. Self-love means the perception and identification of your deepest self. Which raises the essential human question, "Who am I? Am I the public me that goes to work and office parties, or the private me, the sum total of all those deep and dark secrets I keep so carefully hidden?"

Evolutionary mysticism points to a different figure to stand forward when their name is called: the third me, the Unique Self.

The Three Faces

You have three faces. The first face, the social you, is called in the Zohar the "revealed world." Much of capitalist, accomplishment driven, middle-class bourgeois society believes that this first face is the real you. The second face, the primal raging of the subconscious, is called by the Zohar the "hidden world." Freud believed that the real you is the second you, while the outside persona is just the thin veneer of culture. Evolutionary mysticism, however, teaches that your deepest face is your third face—Unique Self—what the Aramaic texts call *Umka De Umka*, the "deepest of the deep"! In the language of Abraham Kook, "The truth of your essence reveals itself in the moment of your greatness."

It is those moments of greatness that set the standard that defines you—that are you. Who you really are is you at your best.

During my first year as a rabbi in Palm Beach, Florida, there was one bar mitzvah boy I will never forget. Louis was his name, and he was the first child to be bar mitzvahed during my tenure. He and his parents came to my office just a few weeks after I arrived, in what turned out to be quite a disturbing meeting. You see, Louis was not a happy camper. He was overweight, awkward, and socially ill at ease—none of these traits easy for a twelve-year-old trapped in the superficiality of a culture that idolized fitness, grace, and cool.

But to add to the taunts of his peers, his parents seemed to be doing their fair share of damage to Louis's self-esteem. The parents informed me, with him in the room, that Louis was not the brightest kid, and that he probably would not be able to read the usual portion from Prophets that were read by other bar mitzvah boys. They figured that it would be enough for him to recite the blessings and be done with it. When they left my office I was bewildered, angry, and near tears. Perhaps it was his parents' insensitivity, or perhaps his awkwardness reminded me of myself at his age. I resolved to do something.

In the ensuing six months, I met with Louis approximately three times as much as I would have met with another bar mitzvah boy. To my extreme delight, I found that Louis had a beautiful singing voice and could do the normal reading from Prophets, but I believed that he could do more. Thus, we trained not only for the Prophets, but the entire biblical reading for the week, no mean feat for a thirteen-year-old by any standard. We practiced and practiced and practiced.

Come the morning of the bar mitzvah, Louis got up, and I tell you that angels carried his every word. He shined! He glowed! The room and the heavens stood still in awe and wonder at the beauty and grace that was Louis. I got up to give the speech that I had prepared, but only one thought filled my mind. I had to speak directly to Louis. I had to make sure he realized the full magnificence—and significance—of that moment. The whole congregation seemed to disappear as I turned to Louis and let the words flow from my mouth: "Louis, this morning you met your real self. You are unique, gorgeous, and beautiful. You are your best. This is who you really are. In this moment, your Unique Self shines with laser-like brilliance. It is who you are. You are good, graceful, talented, and smart. Whatever people told you yesterday, and Louis, whatever happens tomorrow, promise me one thing, remember . . . this is you. Remember, and don't ever lose it." Several months after his bar mitzvah, Louis's family moved away, and I lost track of him. But a few years back I received a letter from Louis. He had just graduated from an Ivy League university, was beginning medical school in the fall, and was engaged to be married. The letter was short. It read, "High school was a nightmare. Sometimes I didn't think I would make it through. But I kept my promise—I always remembered my bar mitzvah morning when you said that this feeling of being absolutely special and beautiful is who I really am. Thank you."

The truth of who you are is you at your best.

Self-Love Is Not Narcissism

The master Menachem Mendel of Kotzk said, "a decent person never deceives others, and a special person never deceives himself."

To say that you are anything less than you at your best—at your most wondrous and beautiful—is to deceive yourself, deceive others, and to deceive God. In the end, though, the greatest deception is to think that you are separate and ordinary.

Whenever I talk to people about self-love—which is, after all, according to most authorities, the most important injunction and the goal of all life—there is always a group that gets upset. It sounds narcissistic, they claim, or it will lead to selfishness.

So let's take a moment to make two clear distinctions. Narcissism is to be in love with your separate self—your mask. This is not a good idea, because sooner or later masks fall off, and then you are left loveless. Self-love is to love your unique interior—your Holy of Holies.

Selfishness is to narrow your circle of caring until it includes only yourself and perhaps those that directly affect your well-being. Selfishness is a narrowing of your identity. That is definitive non-erotic thinking. Self-love, by contrast, is not self-centered at all; it is ultimately expansive.

Self-love is radically erotic in that it is the experience of being interwoven within the great One Taste fabric of being. It is the deep intuition that the world is a unified, loving consciousness in which you participate and which lives in you even as you are an indivisible part of it. To think you are not lovable is the ultimate arrogance, because it says that you are separate from God.

CHAPTER EIGHT

JOY AND UNIQUE SELF

HERE IS THE SIMPLE TRUTH ABOUT JOY: You won't find it in the ways you have learned to search for it all your life. When you pursue joy, it runs away from you.

A student came to his master and said, "Teacher, you taught me that if I run from honor, then honor will pursue me. Well, I have been running from honor for many years now, and honor is still not pursuing me."

"The problem," replied the master, nodding sagaciously, "is clearly apparent. When you run from honor, you are always looking over your shoulder to see if honor is pursuing you—so honor is confused, not quite sure which way you are going."

Joy, like honor and serenity and so much else we ache and sweat for, is only available to us when we actively seek something else instead.

The Babylonian Talmud discusses several wisdom texts that seem to hold contradictory views on joy. One set of passages denies the possibility of achieving true joy, while the second set is far more encouraging.[1]

A resolution is achieved by explaining that the two texts are in fact talking about two different sorts of joy. The first is joy as a detached value—a towering ideal, a castle that rests on an ever-retreating horizon. The second is happiness as a by-product—the ever-present companion that walks with life's meaningful goals. The Talmudic conclusion in a nutshell: joy as a detached value is not achievable; joy pursued as an ideal, for its own sake, will never be attained. Happiness can only be realized as the by-product of the pursuit of some other goal.

What is the primary goal that you must pursue in order to achieve joy as a by-product? Joy is the by-product of your Unique Self-realization. In the normal course of living, you are happy when you are living your Unique Self and unhappy when you are not.

The joy that is a by-product of Unique Self living is called by the myth masters "the joy of mitzvah." Although the word mitzvah is usually translated from the Hebrew as "commandment," the Kabbalists, ever sensitive to the nuances of Hebrew language, understand mitzvah to derive from a root word meaning "intimacy." For us Unique Self seekers, that is a very valuable translation of the word, connecting joy with intimacy. Intimacy is both personal and interpersonal. Intimacy happens when you realize your Unique Self and intertwine it with that of another.

The imperative of biblical consciousness is not "Be joyful." Rather, it is "Choose life"—which in the Biblical myth means choose your life. Live your Unique Self in the world.

"Joyous is the believer," proclaim the biblical-myth masters. The Kabbalists would interpret this declaration to mean, "Joyous is one who believes that they have a unique destiny," a Unique Self. To believe is not to believe that "it" is true, but that "I" am true. When you live your Unique Self, you experience your truth of your existence and are thus freed from the need to affirm it by believing in an external set of dogmas.

"He who is prosperous," teaches the Babylonian wisdom master ben Zoma, "is he who is joyous in his unique part."[2] Usually we understand ben Zoma to mean, "Happiness is to appreciate what you have—unhappiness is to appreciate what you don't have." That is generally sound advice. However, while appreciation is an absolute prerequisite for happiness, it is insufficient by itself to make a person happy.

We can learn from that sort of appreciation, and as we will see, we can move past it into a more sustaining "mere joy." However, appreciation is a very good place to start.

Your Unique Self fits you more perfectly than any tailored suit of clothes. To get up in the morning knowing that you are already clothed in your own uniqueness, that you are doing something in the world totally distinctive to you and you alone, which no one else in the world can do quite like you do—that is mere joy.

The Joy of Depth

If you're essentially on the wrong track, wearing someone else's shoes, leaving someone else's marks, living someone else's print—then there is a level of depth you can never achieve. And what you do achieve will give you far less satisfaction than if you walk a mile, or a lifetime of miles, in your own shoes.

When a person feels their own depth, they are granted a dimension of inner peace, which is the essential prerequisite to authentic joy, and they bring that depth to the surface. We've all heard people say, "Her face was radiant!" or "you're shining!" When inner joy pervades, it emanates from the light of the face.

Ultimately, however, the face is not about hope or despair. It is the primary expression of singularity. The Talmudic myth masters write, "Just as their faces are different, so is their essence."

Indeed, if we do not respond to the call of our destiny—to the *mispar* of our soul's light—if we do not soar as high as we can soar, then we will endanger our fundamental joy.

We have uncovered the evolutionary mystical idea that joy cannot be pursued, that it is only achievable as a by-product of the pursuit of important goals—goals other than happiness itself. What are those goals? Some very good thinkers have suggested that those goals would be something general and admirable, like goodness, depth, values, and meaning. Will following those abstract goals make us happy?

Let's take one of those four goals—values—and see how it plays out. For all of us, there is a gap between the values we profess and the values we practice. By actively pursuing our values, we narrow the yawning gap between our professed and our practiced values, between our happiness and us. Thus, the more we pursue our values, the happier we can be—or so it seems.

You can be good, be deep, possess impeccable values, live a meaningful life, and still be miserable. For there is still one essential element you may be lacking: a profound connection with your Unique Self.

You can buy the best clothes in the world made from the finest fabrics by the most elegant of tailors. If the clothes don't quite fit—and even if you are the only one who notices—they will not give you that joyous feeling that comes from putting on great clothes that fall perfectly on your body. So, too, regarding what the Kabbalah calls the "garments of the soul." These are garments made of your unique goodness, meaning, depth, and values. Garments of that nature are transformative and joy inducing. Happy is the person who wears them.

From Daimon Comes Eudaimonia

The novelist Honoré de Balzac wrote, "Vocations that we wanted to pursue, but didn't, bleed, like colors, on the whole of our existence." If we do not pursue our particular call, then the ghost of that call will pursue us, like a haunting that stains our days.

For when you respond to cues that are not yours, when you're a police officer instead of a painter, ultimately you can't be happy. Happiness comes from being yourself in the most profound way possible. The ancient Greeks referred to happiness as *eudaimonia*. "Daimon" is the word for calling. You are happy only when you are responding to your daimon. Your daimon calls you to realize your Unique Self. Your happiness lies in your hands, if you would but take it.

To be happy, then, is to be responsive to the call of your deepest self. To be happy is to wake up in the morning and feel that you have a mission in the world that no one else can perform. To be happy is to know that among the billions of people on this planet, you are irreplaceable. This is true for every human being on the face of the globe, for what we share in common is our uniqueness.

The Western notion of the sacredness of every human life bursts from the bedrock of the Hebrew myth realization that brings forth the idea of the Unique Self. The prospect of happiness exists for us only because the call of Unique Self animates the Universe.

A Paradigm Shift in Understanding Joy

Joy, teach the Kabbalists, is both a source and a conduit of energy. The word most often associated in Kabbalah with joy is *chiyut*, roughly translated as "life energy," somewhat like the Chinese notion of chi. To be happy is to be plugged into the *chiyut* of the Universe. The portal to that energy is the self, the vital Unique Self. At the same time, once you are plugged in, the joy itself is not only an energy source but also serves as a medium to channel ever-more divine energy.

Joy is more than an attitude; it is a potent and powerful source of energy. The idea of joy as divine energy is expressed by the Kabbalists in many different codes. Let me share one of them with you. A favorite epigram of the Kabbalists is *simcha poretz geder*: "Joy breaks through all fences." One Kabbalist, the master Simcha Bunim (whose first name actually means "happiness"), used this epigram to give a novel explanation of a famous mystical passage, "All the gates are locked, the gates of tears are never locked." Traditionally, this verse has been taken to extol the power of a broken heart to break through all barriers when all other avenues have proven ineffective. When nothing else works, tears can still open all the gates.

In a subtle twist, Simcha Bunim turns the passage on its head: If you are sad, he says, then you can enter only if the gate is unlocked, already wide open. Thus, God has no choice but to leave the gates of tears unlocked. If you are joyous, however, then you can get through even the gates that are locked. After all, *Simcha Poretz Geder*, "joy breaks through all fences."

Choosing Joy

The Kabbalists instruct us that happiness is a decision. In the original mystical language, this idea is expressed in the maxim, "The source of joy is *Binah* (right understanding)." The simple interpretation of that sentence tells us that happiness is accessed through contemplation. One reflects on life and death, sickness, and illness; what is permanent and real; and what is fleeting and illusory. An entire biblical-myth book—Ecclesiastes, or in Hebrew, Kohelet—is devoted to this meditation. "Illusion of illusion, all is illusion," says the king named Kohelet, as he begins his Buddha-like quest for meaning.[3] In the end, he reaches understanding/enlightenment as he finds the inner lining of reality to be made of joy.

The deeper interpretation, however, points to the nature of joy as a *decision*. "The source of joy is right understanding." If joy is a product of understanding, then it is no longer an option or an event or a feeling we await. Joy is a decision. It is a conscious choice. But it is even more than that.

Joy is an obligation.

CHAPTER NINE

THE TEN PRINCIPLES OF UNIQUE SELF SHADOW WORK

"INTEGRATE YOUR SHADOW" HAS BECOME the battle cry of spiritual growth. Shadow integration is now seen as essential to personal development, success, and fulfillment. The centrality of shadow integration in these areas is most certainly a welcome evolution of enormous significance.

The only problem is that people, teachers included, often throw around highly charged words like "darkness" and "shadow" without actually explaining them or having a genuine understanding of what the words actually mean.

The reason the shadow conversation works at all, even without clear understanding, is that people have some natural idea of what "shadow" means. The word "shadow" automatically associates certain images, feelings, and ideas. When Shakespeare talks about "This thing of darkness I acknowledge mine," you understand he is talking about shadow, even if you can't fully articulate it.

Shadow is usually understood to refer to the darker sides of human consciousness. Pettiness, jealousy, betrayal, rage, violence, and malice—these are all considered to be shadow material. Sexual misdeeds are also often associated with the use of the term "shadow."

In this line of spiritual and psychological teaching, "shadow" is explained to mean those qualities that live in you but that you are unable to hold in your first-person consciousness. Your refusal to own these qualities pushes them into shadow, where they exert enormous unconscious influence over your life choices. Some of the shadow teachers add that there is powerful energy in shadow that is—they say— liberated when you make your shadow conscious. Whether or not energy is liberated, and control over your life direction reclaimed by making shadow conscious, is at best not clear. From all my years of teaching, studying, and doing shadow work, I simply do not think it is true. Nonetheless, the explanations for shadow work offered by these teachers are helpful as far as they go. But they do not go nearly far enough. For the *raison d'être* of shadow work is said to be shadow integration.

Why would you want to integrate your darkest impulses? Perhaps those impulses need to be transmuted and evolved. At the very least, it would appear that they need to be disciplined and controlled. Is shadow integration merely a sophisticated license for ethical libertines, as some spiritual moralists have wanted to claim? And if it is not, if shadow integration points to some profound and important intuition about our wholeness and enlightenment, as others have loudly claimed, but not explained, then what is it?

A once-popular spiritual book called *The Book of Qualities* says, "The spiritual practice of shadow encourages us to make peace with those parts of ourselves we find despicable, unworthy, and embarrassing, our anger, jealousy, pride, selfishness, violence, and other evil deeds." The purpose of shadow work is said to be "a way of achieving wholeness by unifying the dark and the light," taking responsibility, and "embracing your full humanity." [1]

What exactly does it mean to unify light and darkness? Did the writer miss Aristotle's law of the excluded middle, which says that opposites do not unify? How do we unify that which is good and that which the writer calls "despicable"? And what does it mean to "embrace" your impulse toward murder, rape, and mayhem as part of your "full humanity"?

Perhaps a little bit of holy war is in order. Is it not possible that making peace with your shadow is just a saccharine way to let you off the hook of the full, powerful, and sacred obligation to evolve out of your darkness and into your light?

This confused understanding of shadow is the rule rather than the exception. For example, a similar approach to shadow is shot through poet Robert Bly's well-known and oft-cited *A Little Book on the Human Shadow.* Though I am a fan of his poetry, his explanation of shadow does not offer us anything near an in-depth understanding of what shadow integration might mean. For Bly, shadow is composed of what you had to suppress as a child to please the grown-ups around you:

> When we were one or two years old we had what we might visualize as a 360-degree personality. Energy radiated out from all parts of our body and all parts of our psyche. A child running is a living globe of energy. We had a ball of energy, all right; but one day we noticed that our parents didn't like certain parts of that ball. They said things like: "Can't you be still?" or "It isn't nice to try and kill your brother." Behind us we have an invisible bad, and the part of us our parents don't like, we, to keep our parents' love, put in the bag. By the time we go to school our bag is quite large. Then our teachers have their say: "Good children don't get angry over such little things." So we take our anger and put it in the bag. By the time my brother and I were twelve in Madison, Minnesota, we were known as "the nice Bly boys." Our bags were already a mile long.

With great respect to Bly, this paradigmatic passage is confusing. What is so bad about going through the ethical socialization required to become a "nice Bly boy"? Is it so heinous to leave behind your attempts to suffocate your brother with a pillow? Isn't growing beyond the murderous rage that spawned the first fratricide a good and noble goal of human evolution? Shouldn't authentic teachers help us discern between legitimate and inappropriate anger? Finally, Bly's implicit idea is regressive in the extreme: The one-or two-year-old with an energy-radiating 360-degree personality.[2]

Naturally, the understanding of shadow integration that I have outlined until this point is not without wisdom. It is true but partial. This teaching assumes that shadow means jealousy, rage, pettiness, violence, and all the other negative ethical expressions. Shadow integration simply means to own the fact that you are jealous, angry, filled with rage, insanely promiscuous, addicted to all forms of comfort, and much more. Bring your disowned shadow into first person. Shadow integration comes to mean something like, "get out of denial and admit that you are an asshole." And free up the energy you have used to cover up being an asshole.

Now, this is not a bad idea. Indeed, it is absolutely critical for any form of spiritual or psychological growth. Someone who owns his or her dark side is generally more tolerable than someone who does not. When you are in denial, you are more dangerous, because it is impossible to engage in authentic conversation around any genuine issue. A good rule of life might be: self-acknowledged assholes are easier and more fun to hang out with than assholes in denial.

This understanding of "owning your shadow," however, might be called more accurately something like shadow confession. So where does the integration piece come in? How do you integrate your shadow, and why would you want to?

Some psychological teachers explain shadow integration as making a place within your own psyche for your rage, envy, greed, dishonesty, and pettiness, so that you do not project them onto everyone else.

This good and important teaching is generally attributed to Carl Jung. Shadow is understood by Jung to be your "dark side," that part of yourself that you hide away—afraid to expose it to the light of day. Shadow is anything that you cannot hold as "I" in your self definition—your less-than-noble qualities, including fear, rage, uncontrolled sexing, envy, greed, egoic pettiness, violence, frustration, depression, and more. It is in this context that Jung wrote, "the most terrifying thing is to accept oneself completely."

Taking back shadow projection is a huge evolutionary leap forward and needs to be taught, practiced, and applauded. It allows for a more honest picture of reality, which always opens the heart up for deeper and more stable loving. But taking back projection still does not explain the core teaching of shadow integration.

Greater Is the Light That Comes from the Darkness

Jung himself offered a more profound direction in understanding shadow. His core teaching, drawn from many sources, is that we cannot be whole human beings without recognizing and incorporating our shadow energy. Jung has an expression that he used to express this idea: "In the shadow is the gold." By this, he means to say that most of what is valuable in the human personality—the gold—can be mined only from the shadow.

At this point, we are ready to unpack the raw outline of this evolutionary mystical teaching of Unique Self/Unique Shadow in the ten principles of shadow work and, in the next chapter, the eight tenets of evolutionary intimacy.

1. Shadow is your Unique Self distortion.

Shadow is not merely your "night virtues"—your lust, fear, anger, jealousy, or envy. This is why the teaching of shadow integration that understands the night virtues as the core of shadow makes so little sense. These night virtues are ethical violations, which, if unrectified, have profound implications for your life and karma. This is the teaching of all the great traditions in the perennial philosophy. The night virtues are obviously shadow qualities, but the night virtues are not the core of shadow. Shadow qualities are not the essence of your shadow but merely an expression of your shadow. Your shadow is the distortion of your Unique Self—the part of your story that is unlived or distorted, and is therefore in darkness. The Hebrew word for story, *sippur* has the same root as one of the great mystical words for light, *sapir*. Your light is your story. Your story is your unique frequency of light. The part of your story that is not lived—that is not in the light—is in darkness. It is that unlived story that is the core of your shadow. Naturally then, the disowning of your unique story creates your Unique Shadow.

2. Your story includes both your True Self and Unique Self.

Your True Self is your freedom, and your Unique Self is your fullness.

Your freedom is beyond all forms: it is your realization of your utter identity with the divine, with All-That-Is. This is your absolute emptiness. You are emptied of all superficial and limiting identities. In this precise sense, you are absolutely free. You are not a-part, separate, and alone, but an indivisible part of the One. This is the realization of classic enlightenment. This is the enlightenment of True Self.

Your fullness is the uniqueness of your play within form: it is the fullness of your unique story, the distinct expression of your divinity, of All-That-Is. Your story is all the unique gifts, pleasures, needs, and obligations that flow from your singular signature. Your story is the evolutionary service that you offer the world, the service that can be done by you and you alone. All of this is the fullness and fulfillment of your Unique Self.

3. Any part of your story that you do not live, lives in darkness.

In your meeting with parents, teachers, culture, and peers, you were wounded. This is true of every human being. It is part of the evolutionary journey. As a result of your hurt, you put part of your story in shadow. You forgot who you were. To come home, you must recover and embrace the memory of your fullest self. It is in this embrace that you overcome the distorting mechanism of what I call your hug formula. Every person has their own hug formula. Your hug formula determines the part of your self that you are willing to disown in order to receive the approval—the hug—that makes you feel like you belong in the world. This part of you becomes unconscious. It lives in shadow. This is your repressed shadow.

There are also parts of you that are unconscious, not because you unknowingly pushed them into shadow, but because they have never seen the light of day. They are unconscious because they have never been conscious. You have not evolved to the full realization of your identity, so it remains in shadow. For example, you may still identify with your isolated separate-self ego. You have not realized your True Self, distinctly expressed as your Unique Self. Any part of your enlightened True or Unique Self that is not realized lives in shadow. This is your developmental or emergent shadow. It is the part of you that has not yet developed or emerged—that is still in shadow.

4. When unique light is trapped in shadow, it does not remain static.

The untold and unlived night stories that are hidden, even from you, always devolve. They fester and fume. They demand to be lived and heard.

Consciousness, energy, and light, like fresh water, are meant to flow. Their nature is dynamic and constantly evolving. For this is the nature of the divine. When light is trapped in shadow, it does not remain static. It becomes stagnant. There is either evolution or devolution. This is the same principle that causes the festering of unexpressed hurt or an untransformed wound.

That which remains unseen either grows or shrinks, but it always changes. That which is unconsciously placed in shadow always devolves.

Once it can be seen and talked of, it can breathe again, and the evolution of your light can resume its normal trajectory. Hidden in shadow does not mean held privately. There are sacred secrets that are appropriately never public, but always held hidden in the love-light of consciousness.

Some sacred secrets must be held privately in order to grow, like seeds under the ground. (One must not confuse sacred secrets with sordid secrets.) But to hide your light from yourself out of fear or shame will cause the light to become dense, distorted, and destructive. Shadow refers to those untold night stories trapped in your unconscious that fester and fume, demanding their day.

5. When unlived life stagnates and devolves, it re-emerges as shadow qualities.

Shadow qualities include addictions of every form—rage, betrayal, envy, jealousy, and more. You do not want to integrate shadow qualities. You want to re-integrate shadow.

Your unlived life is stuffed in the darkness. It stagnates and devolves, and re-emerges as shadow qualities. Until the story of your life is lived, you will go on desperately yearning for it. When your desperate yearning is not nourished by the Eros of your story, it devolves to desperate craving, which is filled by the pseudo-eros of addiction. They are shadow qualities. Once you have realized and integrated your shadow, which is your unlived life, the shadow qualities lose their *raison d'être* and begin to drop away.

Say you are frustrated and angry. You wanted to build a toolshed in the backyard all weekend. This is the life that you need to live on this weekend. It is Sunday evening. You have not built the shed. In your interior, this unlived life makes you feel terrible. You feel incompetent, not powerful, and unable to take care of yourself. You feel like you did not keep your word to yourself. All the other times that you let yourself or someone else down come to the fore of your consciousness. All of these times are part of your unlived life. You did not live the life of the reliable and trusted friend who you truly are. None of this, however, is fully conscious. These feelings are not in the light, because they do not mesh with your self-identity as a person living a life that is good, competent, powerful, and capable. This is shadow material.

Your wife has been away all weekend on a business trip. She returns after she has successfully completed her weekend mission. She walks in the house, gives you a hug, and asks, "Honey, how was your weekend? Did you get that shed built?" Her tone is innocent, but you do not hear it that way. You explode with rage at her. You get angry with her for daring to be so frustrated and upset with you.

Shadow in this example is a Unique Shadow, which emerged from the unlived life that you needed and wanted to live that weekend.

What happened? There are several distinct steps. You are frustrated and angry with yourself for not having fulfilled your commitment. The life that was yours to live at that time was "to build the shed." But you do not consciously "own" your frustration and anger for failing to live your life. You especially want to distance yourself from your feeling of being inadequate, not enough, or bad.

Your partner's innocent question unleashes a swamp of hidden bad feelings in regard to your unlived life and brings them to the surface. You naturally do not want to direct these feelings against yourself, but they need to be directed somewhere. So you turn your anger against your partner. This is the first level of what is going on.

On an even deeper level, you are engaged in projection. You project all of your own frustration and anger with yourself onto your partner. For that very reason, you experience *her* as being angry and frustrated with you. You then proceed to get angry with her for daring to be so frustrated and upset with you.

Your unlived life—the project you wanted to finish—has been disowned and placed into shadow. There it devolved into rage, anxiety, and frustration. All of these shadow qualities were then projected onto your beloved partner.

If you would enter the inside of your anger, it would lead you back to your own desire to build the shed. Building the shed in a timely and effective manner was the expression of your Unique Self on that particular weekend. Actually building the shed would be the way to follow your Unique Shadow back to your Unique Light.

Let me give you two more examples of the Unique Self–Unique Shadow complex.

Unlived Passion

About a decade ago I spent several years working with a woman named Amelia. Amelia was the dean and a teacher of comparative religion at a prestigious private school for girls in Europe. She was a cultured, ethical, compassionate woman of considerable depth and insight, with a balanced and delightful disposition. The explicit goal of our work was to facilitate Amelia's Unique Self enlightenment. Amelia had this quite unexpected habit of getting into very embroiled verbal fights with her colleagues over seemingly nonsensical issues. She would take a position on an apparently innocuous matter, and then fight for it with a passion and vehemence that was way out of proportion to the nature of the issue at hand. This made little sense to Amelia or to myself. It was troubling not only because it caused her no small amount of grief, but also because it was so completely out of character. Our breakthrough moment in regard to this issue came from the realization, which was then growing in me, that Unique Shadow is always the road back to Unique Self. During our work together, one of our major focal points was Amelia as a teacher. In order to confirm an intuition that had been brewing in me, I asked her to "teach me" several classes, with me as the student. She did. The classes were lovely, nuanced, and insightful.

But something was wrong. The quality of her teaching was profoundly feminine, in that it held space for everyone, received everyone's feedback, and sought to validate the opinions of all the students. But it was not compelling. It lacked the passion needed to penetrate the heart. The quality of masculine insemination that plants a great idea forever in the heart and mind of a young person was strikingly absent. Now, this was not because Amelia lacked passionate beliefs or deeply held certainties. She did not lack these things. But as it emerged, she was enculturated in the progressive ethos of teaching that viewed masculine passion and insemination as a violation of the autonomy of the student. It confused ecstasy with frenzy, and transmission of a truth with intellectual domination. In this ethos, the role of the teacher was virtually always that of facilitator and virtually never that of passionate inseminator. As a result, Amelia was never able to convey the depth of her teaching and deeply held knowing to her students. Her Unique Self as a teacher remained both unlived and distorted.

What naturally happened then was that Amelia's distorted Unique Self appeared as Amelia's Unique Shadow. Her petty fights filled with passion and fervor over irrelevant issues were but the unlived vocation of the passionate, compelling teacher showing up in shadow form. Once this became clear to us, Amelia began to shift her teaching style significantly, and within six months, the nasty fights that had dogged her career and relationships disappeared almost entirely. She evolved from being the lovely, nice teacher to the compelling, provocative teacher. Much to her surprise and delight, her popularity soared. Amelia had followed her Unique Shadow back to her Unique Self.

Taking Anger into Account

A second story involves a student from southern Israel who came to me because he had a terrible problem with anger. He was angry with his kids, his wife, and himself most of the time. I tried every kind of anger management technique I knew and more for a period of many months. Nothing worked.

By profession, he was an accountant. He was also a man who had, from the time he was very young, a deep passion for social justice. After several weeks of talking, I shocked him by telling him I thought he should leave accounting and run for mayor of his small town. His wife was particularly aghast at the prospect. He made a good, stable living as an accountant, and was often home and available (if angry) for her and the kids. Why give this up for the financial and social vagaries of political life?

I shared with both of them my intuition, which had come to me in a flash in the midst of a late-night prayer. I sensed that his anger was not based on old childhood issues or any kind of character disorder. Rather, it was the sublimated anger of protest, of a leader and revolutionary trapped in an office adding up numbers for other people.

Now, being an accountant is a wonderful, honorable, and vitally needed profession—but not if you are a revolutionary! A few years and many ups and downs later, he in fact became the mayor of his town. To his and his family's surprise, what had been his petty and unpredictable bouts of rage simply stopped. He became a different person. He stepped into his Unique Self, so his shadow—his distorted or unlived Unique Self—naturally disappeared. In this case, the anger itself was re-channeled and vitally transformed. It remained passionate, but lost its bitter and sometimes mean sense, and took on a cleaner and even compassionate quality.

The path of transformation of identity teaches that only through using your Unique Shadow as a guide to Unique Self can you ever find your way back to your story.

6. You feel the full depth of the goodness and aliveness of your life only when you are fully living your full story.

When you are not living your full story, you do not feel that you fully exist. You do not feel adequate, dignified, or valuable. Anything less than your unique and special story makes you feel unworthy. The feeling of emptiness that always accompanies the feeling of unworthiness is the source of every form of addiction and acting out. Stories, of course, have many layers, plots, and subplots. You may feel the fullness of your story in one dimension of your life, and you may feel drab and adrift in other parts of your life. This is how you know where your story, your Book of Life, needs editing or rewriting.

If you're not living your story, you create a pseudo-story. If you're not in your Eros, you are seduced by pseudo-eros and false stories. You fill up your emptiness with snakes and scorpions—all the shadow qualities, all the night virtues, all the addictions. Once your unlived life is in darkness, it undergoes degradation. You feel numb and empty. You unconsciously reach out for something to cover the emptiness. You cast about for depth and fulfillment, which can only be truly found by reclaiming your unlived life.

Often anger supplies you with a hit of pseudo-fullness. But since your internal self-image is that of a contented and successful person, you cannot own your anger. Unwarranted anger is a shadow quality. Your disowned anger remains in your space, but since your anger is not in you, you project it onto others, who you then think are angry with you. You then become sad because you feel that people are angry with you. Over time this turns into a low-grade depression. And the cycle continues its downward degenerative spiral of unlove and alienation. When you are miscast, you cast about. You act out when you are the leading actor in the wrong script. You can only receive an Oscar for playing a starring role in your own life. Being in the wrong story creates massive interior pain, which in turn gives birth to your shadow qualities.

7. Shadow is a lie about your Unique Self. Shadow is a lie about your essential identity.

When you lie about your life, you create shadow qualities. It takes enormous energy to support a lie. This is especially true when it is not a "detail lie" about this or that, but a lie about the very fabric of your identity. You deny ownership of essential voices in your self. You hide those parts of you that challenge the image of the man or woman you want and claim to be. You do not have an accurate picture of yourself. Because this is so, you cannot accurately judge how to interact with others.

Since you have edited out or plagiarized part of your story, you do not feel whole or authentic. On the contrary, you feel desiccated and fraudulent. You feel fragmented. You feel like an impostor waiting to be found out.

In order to reclaim your story, you must accept authorship and ownership of all of your narrative. Authorship is the source of authority. Only the author of your life story has control over the destiny and destination of your narrative. You must go back to your Book of Life, and see when you started either editing or plagiarizing your life script. Your shadow consists of the parts of your story that have been left on the cutting-room floor. They are screaming to get your attention, so that you will re-include them in the story of your life.

Let me give a startling illustration of this principle. Every human being is a precisely unique balance of masculine and feminine. The precise calibration of these two qualities is unique in every human being. No two hermaphrodites are the same. To the precise extent that these qualities are imbalanced or not expressed, the essential truth of your Unique Self is violated. You are living a lie. Any part of your masculine or feminine that is unlived, imbalanced, or distanced will create shadow. The lie of your shadow will ultimately express itself in your acting out in shadow qualities.

8. Shadow integration does not mean to integrate shadow qualities. Shadow integration does mean to reclaim your unlived life that is in darkness.

A popular teaching on shadow suggests that by integrating your shadow, you will gain the advantage of the shadow energy. But it is more than unclear what this means. How do you integrate the energy of murder? Murderous energy explodes, and then dissipates. This is energy without depth or stability.

The energy of murder, at its core, stems from your own disconnection with the fullness of your Unique Self. Shadow integration means to reclaim your unlived life and thereby reclaim your life force. The energy you reclaim with shadow integration is the full force, power, and vitality of your Unique Self, directed not toward destruction but toward creativity, compassion, and Eros.

9. Joy is your life energy. Joy is a by-product of Unique Self living.

Joy, as we have seen, is realized as the natural by-product of the passionate pursuit of something other than happiness.

What is that other thing that you pursue passionately that is not joy, that is a by-product of its pursuit? Of course, you must pursue virtue, goodness, integrity, depth, values—all necessary, but insufficient to give you joy. It's not just virtue, goodness, integrity, and depth that you need to pursue; you must pursue *your* virtue, goodness, integrity, and depth— that is to say, your story.

Joy is a by-product of living your story.

The Chinese taught us that joy is chi, joy is energy. In Hebrew mysticism, joy is called *chiyut*, which means "vital energy," or "life force." so both the Chinese tradition and the Hebrew mystical tradition use virtually the same root word to allude to joy.

Once you understand all of this clearly, the imperative to integrate shadow makes sense once again. When you reclaim your unlived life and weave it back into the fabric of your sacred autobiography, you bring joy— energy—back into your life. Your Unique Self is the portal to your joy. You move from being depleted to being energized. Where you once were listless, you are now full of vigor. Valium gives way to vitality.

When all the principles we have enumerated until this point are brought together, you realize that there are five progressive steps of life destruction that are the direct result of the Unique Self distortion, which creates Unique Shadow. Each one of these steps drains your life energy in its own particular way. Their successive and cumulative impact on your life is nothing less than devastating. The healing comes directly from the evolution of your identity to your original and unique wholeness. Wholeness is the integration of your unlived life, your True Self and Unique Self, which are acting out as shadow.

1. Your story is your light. Your unlived life-light is shadow. If you take part of your story, part of the Unique Self that you are here to live, which creates your joy, and you put it in shadow, what have you done? You have taken a huge part of your *chiyut* energy and put it in darkness. You have lost the core of your life energy, which remains trapped in your unlived life. This is the essence of the matter. The natural joy-energy of your life, which is a by-product of living your Unique Self, is not available when your core story is in shadow. Your energy and joy are a by-product of the lived fullness of your unique life. You are fully alive and aflame only in your story and your life.

2. Without this core energy, you feel empty. You are left depleted, exhausted, and horribly depressed. Depression further drains your energy.

3. That unlived life that you placed into darkness then devolves and becomes shadow qualities. It devolves into unbridled rage, damaging lust, malice, jealousy, embezzlement, and violence. This further drains your life force.

4. You lose your core alignment with the ecstatic evolutionary impulse of the cosmos that moves toward higher and higher levels of complexity, consciousness, and love. This further drains you of your joy, and hence of your energy and your life force.

5. When your story is in shadow, you must expend enormous energy to maintain the lie about it. To maintain a constant and unnatural lie demands an enormous reserve of energy. This is a further source of your energy loss.

10. The technology for shadow integration is love. Shadow integration effects a transformation of identity. Love is the evolutionary force that transmutes shadow to light.

The inner magic and mechanism of love makes it the ultimate technology of Unique Shadow transformation. The nature of that magic and mechanism is an essential understanding necessary for your Unique

Self enlightenment. In order to integrate your shadow a transformation of your identity must occur. The key Aramaic phrase used by the Unique Self masters to describe the nature of this transformative path is *be'chavivut talya milta*, "it depends on love."

EVOLUTIONARY INTIMACY

The Seven Laws of Unique Self Encounters

Seen from one perspective, life is a series of encounters with other human beings. Of these encounters, the ones that are most profound, pleasurable, and transformative are Unique Self encounters. The following are seven core rules that define a Unique Self encounter:

1. In every Unique Self encounter, each person holds a piece of the other's story, which must be returned to the other in order for both to be complete.

Every person you meet—in a significant meeting—possesses a piece of your story. Some people may have a sentence, others a missing word, while still others may hold a paragraph or even a whole chapter. Significant meetings involve Unique Self encounters.

The ultimate Unique Self encounter may well be with your significant other in life. The person you choose should be the person who can return to you a significant piece of your story, which you have either lost or never found. Conversely, you hold and need to return the missing and magnificent pieces of their story to them. The Unique Self relationship is the committed, caring, dynamic process of discovering just what these missing pieces might be, and puzzling them back together.

A Unique Self encounter, however, is in no sense limited to romantic partners or long-term connections. Others may have pieces of your story, and you of theirs. Nor are Unique Self encounters limited to your sphere of colleagues, friends, family, neighbors, employers, and employees. A Unique Self encounter may last a minute or a lifetime. You may be riding an elevator with a person you have never met and will never meet again, both of you inching up to the twenty-third floor, and somewhere in your casual conversation there will be an important message for each of you. Similarly, the person who returns your lost wallet may have more to give back to you than your credit cards.

There is a Unique Self ethos that cannot be externally enforced or legislated, yet it demands a far higher moral standard than passive public morality. When you have an encounter with another person, you are called on to ask yourself, "Have you brought your Unique Self to the table in the encounter?" And when a Unique Self encounter that should have taken place does not, then we have committed a Unique Self misdemeanor—sometimes even a felony. No one will ever know—except for you, God, and possibly the person with whom you failed to have an encounter.

A Unique Self encounter may be a wisdom encounter. Through your Unique Self convergence with someone, you gain a deeper insight into your own unique pleasure, joy, obligation, need, or shadow. A Unique Self encounter can also be action oriented. You and the person you encounter may be agents of change for each other, each of you provoking the other to do something in the world you never otherwise could have done. Encounters take place between teachers and students, between lovers, among friends, in casual acquaintance, or in chance meetings.

2. To have a Unique Self encounter, you have to make authentic contact in the present.

The second law of Unique Self relationship is that to have a Unique Self encounter, you have to make authentic contact. Without contact with the Unique Self of the other, no encounter may happen. It is for this reason that Unique Self encounters can take place only in the present. Contact is only possible in the present. The only place your story is ever happening is right now.

Yesterday's and tomorrow's story help shape your identity today. This is as it should be. But presence—showing up as your God-self, your Unique Self—is possible only in the present. When you think you are talking to me but you are really completing an unfinished conversation with your mother from years ago, contact cannot be made.

Interaction is the opposite of reaction. Reaction comes from an unconscious re-play, re-hash, and re-living of moments long dead and done. You cannot live a dead moment. Unconscious re-enactment is precisely what psychology calls transference. You are transferring your reactions from an old situation to the present situation, even though they do not apply.

You must enter the inside of the present moment, which is the Unique Self of time. The interaction is in the interface between two people who are face-to-face.

Often, in a potentially intimate encounter, when an inner discomfort arises, that feeling of discomfort has many layers and often arises from our reactions to past events. The discomfort both blocks the process and offers a doorway into the Unique Self in that moment. So one way to deepen contact in an interpersonal encounter is to identify the discomfort present in a particular moment. Stay in the discomfort. Feel into it, and let it well up. Do nothing to dispel it. If you stay in it, even for fifteen minutes, you will feel something new, something deeper arising. As the energy of discomfort is released, a feeling of fullness and well being can arise. This is the essence that lies just beneath your personality, ready to reveal itself.

A Unique Self encounter occurs when the essence of one personal being touches the essence of another personal being, without ego boundaries and without loss of the unique individuation of each unique partner.

A Unique Self encounter requires contact with the person in front of you in the uniqueness of the present moment. One of the well-known teachings in biblical myth states this principle: "Therefore shall a man leave his father and mother and cleave intimately to his wife."

If you look at the text from a psychological viewpoint, you see that it is not just a formal recommendation of marriage. It points to a primal truth about relationship. You cannot create true intimacy without leaving behind, in a psychological sense, your parents. If you do not leave your parents behind, you marry them. You marry someone similar to, or the opposite of, your parents, in order to finish your unfinished business with them. Through that person who is similar to dad, you seek to receive the love you didn't get from dad. Or through that person who is the opposite of mom, you seek to run away from mom. In either case, you are in a relationship, not with your partner, but with your parents. There is no Unique Self encounter.

Contact only takes place in the present, in the Unique Self of the present moment in time. You think you are in the present relating to your partner. Really you are in the past, arguing or pleading with a parent. In this situation, the energy and wisdom that you need to be intimately present with your partner is unavailable.

The Pain Trance

Our inability to remain present is the source of most of our pain and dysfunction. We fail to meet the challenges of each moment not because we lack the resources, but because we allow encounters in the present to trigger past experiences of pain.

An example: Jonathan is up for review at work and the boss says to him, "I think you have potential, but your work is still sloppy. Get that together and you have a great future here." Rather than hearing the promise in his boss's words, Jonathan hears rejection. He gets angry with his boss and feels that the critique was unfair. This causes him to feel so depressed that he later gets into a vociferous argument with his partner about nothing. Or he may call an old romantic partner up for dinner, and inappropriately sleep with her in order to cover the emptiness opened up by his boss's critique. Or he may start a binge of excessive drinking, which in the end causes him to lose the job he held so dear.

What happened here? Essentially, his boss's words triggered old reactions. Jonathan slipped into a trance that took him out of the present moment and threw him into the past. His fastidious father used to shout at him when his room wasn't clean. Dad would go into a rage and call him "a worthless, sloppy mess." Jonathan remembers that phrase. It is indelibly imprinted on his soul. So when someone critiques him as being sloppy, even if it is in the context of great praise and even with a promise for the future, all Jonathan can hear in his subconscious is "worthless and sloppy." He probably does not consciously associate his boss's critique with that ancient moment in his life. He may not even consciously remember his father's words. Yet whenever something or someone presses certain internal triggers, he regresses to those early childhood moments and responds as he did then. This is precisely the image of "pressing buttons." He is in a trance, acting not in the present but in response to old pain.

We all have trances. A trance means simply that you leave the present moment and enter another time or dimension. Daydreaming can be a pleasant version of such a trance. A second example is what psychological literature calls spontaneous age regression. This can also be pleasant, as when the taste of banana slices in cheerios returns you to the feeling-state of a sweet Saturday morning in childhood.

Jonathan's experience, however, is a typical example of negative age regression—what I call a "pain trance." Because it is unconscious, it takes Jonathan out of the present. Because he is not aware that the past is coming up again, he also lacks the presence to heal the past.

Staying in the Present

The most important identifying characteristic of a trance is the distortion of time. You are taken out of the present and regressed to an earlier, more unconscious time in your life. Psychologist Stephen Wolinsky calls this kind of age-regressed unconscious experience a deep trance phenomenon. All such trances are triggered by a narrowing of focus. This is precisely what happens, for example, in most phobias or anxiety attacks. Our focus shrinks to the extent that the rest of the world feels completely cut off. We narrow our focus to a specific image, word, or sensation that effectively blocks out all other words, images, or emotions. In the story we began with, it was the word "sloppy" that became the involuntary mantra of the trance.

At such moments, we forget our larger selves. We don't see options or resources that are right in front of us. We become virtually paralyzed, and cannot change our course of action.

Essentially, the trance takes you out of the present moment. In the mystical understanding of time, the present moment contains everything you need for healing and health, so by leaving it, you are bound to get sick and hurt. Therefore, the goal of spiritual therapeutic intervention should be to return the client to the presence of the present moment. Remember, a trance that takes you out of the present and prevents a Unique Self encounter is usually a return to the childlike reaction that we used to protect ourselves from trauma long ago. Any event that is too painful for the child to integrate is met by a childhood trance.

Let's say, for example, that your mother was verbally abusive. If you responded defensively to her abuse, she would either hit you or scream in an even more frightening and insane way. Your protective trance response was a combination of two internal movements. First, you would watch—without noticing that you were watching—your mother very carefully. This allowed you to anticipate her moods and try to be out of the way when the trauma-spewing volcano erupted. In watching your mother, you would gather all of her misdeeds, much like a prosecuting attorney. Then when she started yelling, you would list off silently to yourself all of her faults. By the time she finished yelling, you had the mental satisfaction of having tried and indicted her in the courtroom of your mind.

Later on in life, when you would get into an argument with your partner, something about it might spontaneously and unconsciously regress you back to your encounters with your mom. This would then elicit in you a withering attack on your partner. You might now have a terrible knack of bringing up all sorts of details you had noticed, and using them to bash your spouse. When your outburst is over, you are ashamed, but the damage is done. The retaliation you used to do mentally to your mother, you now do out loud to your spouse. However, having cultivated the art of careful watching, your outbursts are profoundly more insightful, and therefore more devastating.

These outbursts have been a primary cause of your inability to create lasting, intimate relationships with either friends or a romantic partner. The root of this challenge, which has devastated so much of your life, is your tendency to go into the age-regressed trance state, which takes you out of the present. One purpose of your spiritual practice is to help you remain in the present. In the present, you have all the resources you might need for healing and intimacy. But before you can stay in the present, you first have to learn to catch yourself going into trance.

To Walk in the Wide Places

Stephen Wolinsky tells the story of a client named Clare. She was a binge drinker, and before one of these binge episodes, she would first slip into an invisible trance. She would get very tight, create distance between herself and the world, and would not fully see the people around her—they would seem to blur out of focus. Her normal level of unease in the world would quickly become more pronounced, and she could only think about having a drink.

This was the strategy Clare used to survive childhood abuse. She would shut out her external environment. The abuser would shift out of focus, and she would withdraw into her own world. Wolinsky writes, "in my break through moment I realized that in order for her to create the distance she needed to survive as a child, she had to not see much of her immediate external environment." She would withdraw and enter—entrance—her own world.

What provokes this reaction in us later in life is virtually always the meeting with something or someone that triggers our core unique wound. We are suddenly and unconsciously thrown back to that early place where we first met the emptiness and the wound.

Our sense of our goodness in early childhood depends on our caretakers serving as a conduit for the Universe's loving embrace. When those love vessels are constricted and narrowed, our soul feels attacked. We then withdraw into our contracted-ego small-self for self-protection. This prevents the pain of the emptiness from drowning us. We only shut down when the pain overloads our circuits; instead of blowing our system, we turn off. We withdraw—no longer present in the present. When meeting with "emptiness" in the present, it often evokes this old challenge to our self-worth. We slip into a "past" without ever noticing the slippage. Thinking we are in the past, the same set of survival strategies kick in. We withdraw into whatever our unique trance patterns are—and look for a way to navigate the emptiness without being swallowed up.

In childhood, such an event is always interpersonal—that is, a reaction to another person or people outside of ourselves. But in adulthood, when the reactive mechanism is triggered, it kicks in autonomously—that is, without it being a protective strategy against a real person. Anything that sets off our emptiness barometer returns us to the place of original unhealed trauma where we encountered the wound originally. We then react—automatically and unconsciously—as we did then.

Staying in the Symptoms

What Wolinsky brilliantly noticed was that in telling the story of the symptom, the trance was re-induced. What that meant to him—in a simple yet elegant insight—was that if he could help his client short-circuit the trance in the telling of the story, then the client would be able to short-circuit the trance when it kicked in at other times. The key is to pay attention and notice when trance symptoms are kicking in. The critical assumption is that the negative behavior can kick in only after the trance and as a direct result of it. Short-circuit the trance, and nine times out of ten you have short-circuited the destructive behavior.

Wolinsky also tells of a young woman who comes to therapy with the problem of not being able to have an orgasm. She knows that her stepfather molested her at age nine. One could engage a long and complex process of "working through" the abuse. Or, in a far more direct and effective approach, the trained therapist or guide might say something like, "Jill, when you are having sex, at that moment that you go numb, or freeze up, or space out, get a picture of that moment and describe it for me."

While recreating her symptom trance, Jill might answer slowly, "my shoulders are tight . . . my jaw is tight . . . my stomach is tight . . . I'm holding my breath . . . I'm thinking to myself, 'Don't touch me, don't come near me, don't hurt me.' "

"All right, Jill," the therapist continues, "What I'd like you to do is to merge with the picture . . . continue to hold your muscles tightly while you breathe and look at me."

This is the pivoting point. The therapist says to Jill, "Stay with your trance symptoms but don't disappear. Stay here with me." A trance is almost always induced in part by a shift in normal breathing. In many sacred languages, the word for "breath" has the same root, or is even the same word, as the word for "soul." In biblical myth, God fashions the human being through an act of inspiration: "God breathed into man the breath of life." This breath of life is the loving flow of divine life-energy in the Universe. In trauma, this loving flow is cut off, reflected in a tightening in the chest, or other shifts in breathing. In reconnecting to the breath, you reconnect to the life force.

In this case, establishing a loving and trusting relationship allows the client to move through the trance symptoms and reconnect with the loving breath of the Universe. By doing so, the trance is short-circuited.

In light of all this, let's reread the spiritual principle of biblical myth with which we began: "Therefore shall a man leave his father and mother and cleave intimately to his wife."

There are two steps. Step one: You need to *de-trance*. Those meetings with emptiness that cause spontaneous age regression need to be short-circuited. You need to move beyond old conversations with father and mother. Here father and mother are, of course, only symbols of the formative relationships of our early years.

Step two: Having become *de-tranced*, you can now create intimacy with your partner. A Unique Self encounter is now possible. You are in the present, with the person in front of you—not a figure from the past. Contact can be made.

3. Labels obstruct contact.

Labels can be anything from "smart," "stupid," "beautiful," or "ugly," to words noting race or religious affiliation or role designation. A label is naturally illuminating when it describes or conveys important information about the object or subject being labeled, like properly labeled medicine. A label is blinding when it prevents your attention from actually settling directly on the object or subject that you are encountering. It is this kind of label that obstructs authentic contact between Unique Selves.

Janis did her internship at Bellevue Hospital on the locked psychiatric ward. After her first session, she hurried to leave the ward to get to class at NYU. When she went up to the guard and asked to be let out, he looked at her with a slightly surprised smile and asked, "What do you mean? I'm not going to let you out!"

Janis was a little bewildered by his answer, but tried to explain.

"I'm a student at NYU and have to get to class. Can you please let me out?"

He laughed at her again incredulously. "Yeah, right! And I'm the dean of Harvard Law School. I can't let you out!"

Janis suddenly realized she was stuck in a locked ward, and that anything she said would not be believed. She was locked in the guard's conception of her as a patient!

Finally, after some panicked moments, she found a supervisor on the ward and told him what had happened. He looked at her, suppressing a smile, and asked, "But Janis, why were you asking a patient to let you out?"

Positive or negative, every blinding label builds walls. When you hold on to your labels and self-definitions ("I'm not good at this; I could never do that"), you refuse to treat yourself as a full human being with infinite potential. When you give labels to other people or types of people ("She's bad with numbers," "She's a narcissist and can never heal"), you estrange yourself from other people's Unique Selves. You are no longer able to make contact.

The most often mentioned ethical guideline in biblical mysticism— appearing no less than thirty-six times—is, "Deal kindly with the stranger." A stranger is anyone whose Unique Self is blocked from view by a limiting label. This might be a label of their place of origin, family, nationality, or religion. It might be a carelessly affixed label of their ability or potential. Limiting labels often can refer to physical characteristics or psychological typologies of virtually any kind.

It is not that third-person descriptions, definitions, and categorizations are not helpful. They are. Accurate diagnosis in every field of endeavor is essential to wise and compassionate interaction, whether that is with your doctor, psychologist, romantic partner, or friend. There is a particular form of spiritual consciousness that resists or rejects all labels with the argument that you can do or be whatever you want, and labels simply serve to box you in. This is a partial truth, but like all partial truths, it is also a partial lie. Labels illuminate, reveal, and guide. But as much as they disclose and divulge, labels also obscure and obfuscate, and therefore stand against Unique Self encounters.

You often label compulsively to feel a sense of control and comfort in a situation. Naturally, these labels are often sloppy, inaccurate, or just plain false. A false label will yield false conclusions, which will lead to wrong and destructive action. The simplest example is the destructive, heartrending result of labeling a child retarded or unteachable. At the same time, an accurate diagnosis of a learning disability might lead to wonderfully constructive interventions that heal hearts and open minds. In Unique Self enlightenment, the absolute demand is to never let external labels transform the other into a stranger.

Labeling happens all the time, even when we don't think we are doing it. We label ourselves, as well, in subtle and pernicious ways. "There is no possible way I could ever do that," someone might say about an ambition or desire. That kind of sentiment is a kind of label that estranges us from ourselves. Such comments are certainties that lie. We hold them because they allow us a comfort zone in which we do not need to challenge our self-perceptions or stretch to the fullness of our Unique Selves. Labels are the archenemy of Unique Selves. Relying on labels is like trying to take someone's fingerprint when they are wearing a Band-Aid.

4. You never know.

The goal of Unique Self consciousness is to fully receive and be received in deep understanding and empathy. Yet how often are we simply unable to understand one another? Receiving each other becomes next to impossible because of distance, strangeness, hurry, deafness, carelessness, or inevitable differences in the languages of our Unique Selves. Try as we might, the Unique Selves of so many people are ultimately unknowable to us—just like the Unique Self of God.

Are we to give up, or is there a path of receiving what is true even when you cannot fully grasp the Unique Self of other? And is there a way that another can honor you in your Unique Self even if they cannot fully receive you in understanding and empathy? Is there a way to receive what seems so unreceivable, whether human or divine? This quandary inspires one of the more subtle ideas of St. Thomas Aquinas, the medieval writer who did so much to define Christianity, and of Moses Maimonides, perhaps the most important Jewish philosopher of the last thousand years.

For theologians like Aquinas and Maimonides and many others past and present, the very essence of God is God's incommunicability. According to these two medieval philosophers, God is unknowable. In the language of one scholar, "If I knew him, I would be him." And yet at the same time, they held that the *summum bonum* of human existence is to know God.

But how can you know the one who is not knowable? Aquinas and Maimonides proposed an ingenious solution, which they called via negative or "the affirmation of not knowing"—that is, we know God in acknowledging that we do not know God. In the words of one of French writer Edmond Jabès's characters, "I know you, Lord, in the measure that I do not know you." It is in the same way the Unique Self mystics teach that we receive another even if we do not know them; the Unique Self encounter takes place through the affirmation of not knowing.

For years, I thought the "affirmation of not knowing" was a classic example of irrelevant if clever medieval sophistry. Until on a rare stormy day in Jerusalem, I made my way through the rain to the small neighborhood grocer right next to my house to pick up some essentials for my bad-weather hibernation. A gust of smoke greeted me at the door. The source of the noxious fumes, I soon found out, was a swarthy-faced middle-aged man, loitering in my corner store! Shirt open to the chest, large gold necklace and all, he stood there smoking his 9 a.m. cigar.

Coughing and fanning my way through his smoke, I mumbled to the grocer my consternation at the torrential rains that had soaked me through and through, trying to hide my growing annoyance at this obviously uncouth and obnoxious loiterer.

And then, ever so slowly, the man with the gold necklace turned and looked at me—I promise—with the gentlest look you could possibly imagine. All his features suddenly appeared handsome and majestic. The gold necklace seemed regal, the smoke sweet as an incense offering. "Don't you know," he said, "it's raining today because a holy man has gone to his world." I felt like some gate had swung open inside of me. Something in my heart just fell open—I just wanted to reach out and hug him for being so beautiful. It was an epiphany pure and simple.

Only later when I got home and read the paper did I see that one of Jerusalem's great mystics had in fact died that morning—the Rebbe of Gur, a Hasidic master and leader of a thriving community with origins in the eastern European town of Gur, a community that had been virtually wiped out during the Holocaust. This master had slowly, painstakingly, and with endless love, passion, and daring, rebuilt his community in Israel over the past forty years. The world felt darker without him.

I had totally misjudged the man at the grocer's. I thought he was a boor— coarse and crass, involved only in his immediate needs. However, the shining beauty and the subtle and deep knowing on his face as he told me that a holy man had died let me know how superficial my vision had been. I had assumed I knew him, and I had not truly known him at all. I had not received him.

"You never know—you never know—you never know." A Unique Self encounter is only possible in the felt humility of not knowing. And realizing that at the end of all knowing is—not knowing.

The temptation to label, categorize, dismiss, or otherwise try to put another person in a box is the desire for conquest through knowing. People in boxes threaten us less. Instead, we must seek to receive another's Unique Self, even as we are aware that the other remains mysterious to us, ultimately unknowable, just like God. We are called to honor the Unique Self by gently saying to ourselves, "You never know—you never know—you never know."

5. Unique Self encounters create evolutionary We Space.

Meaningful Unique Self encounters foster the experience of entering together into higher states of awareness and intelligence. The next evolutionary leap in consciousness involves a recognition that, together, we have access to a collective wisdom and intelligence that is much smarter than our individual intelligence.

This is, in a sense, something the mystics have always known: the whole is so much greater than the sum of its parts. What is "new" is that nowadays, in workshops and retreats, in corporate boardrooms and organizational development seminars, as well as in spiritual groups, so many people are experimenting with engaging the phenomenon of collective intelligence.

Here's how it works: a room full of people with clarity of intention come together with focused attention. They engage a challenge, seek a solution, or reach for deeper direction. They seek something precious that was previously unavailable to any of the individuals in the room. It was also unavailable through the classic collaborative methods of sharing information and comparing notes. They use certain group technologies to create a group consciousness within which a new space of insight is revealed. The insight that comes forward often has a visionary wisdom that exceeds the limitations of any of the individuals in the room. Something happens in the center of the room.

The "voice" that rises in the center of such a group, whether in an organizational setting or a spiritually oriented one, is the voice of an emergent higher intelligence. It is the voice of the "whole." All the distinct parts are held, heard, and honored, yet the whole transcends them into the larger love-intelligence that speaks in, as, and through each of us, even as it calls from beyond us. It is from this precise space that collective intelligence wells up.

The famed basketball coach Phil Jackson, who brought the LA Lakers and Chicago Bulls to multiple championships, was explicitly referring to this phenomenon when he talked about "the subtle interweaving of the players at full speed to the point where they are thinking and moving as one."

One participant in a collective consciousness exercise describes it as follows:

> When someone else spoke, it felt as if I were speaking. And when I did speak, it was almost egoless, like it wasn't really me. It was as if something larger was speaking through me. . . . And in that space we started to create. We started to say things that we had never thought before.

Ralph Waldo Emerson writes of this phenomenon: "All are conscious of attaining to a higher self-possession. It shines for all."

In Jewish mysticism, this is called the voice of the Shekhinah—the feminine face of the divine, which in the Hindu traditions is called Shakti. Jewish mystics who wrote in the third century taught, "Whenever ten people gather with clear holy intention, the Shekhinah speaks." Or as Matthew said, "When two or three gather in my name I am in the midst of them." Modern Hindu Mystic Aurobindo called this "the evolution of truth consciousness in which [they] feel themselves to be the embodiment of a single self." Theosophist Rudolf Steiner said, "people awake through each other . . . then real communal spirituality descends on our workplace." Finally, the French Jesuit Teilhard de Chardin, one of the key founders of modern evolutionary spirituality, describes this collective spiritual awakening as "sustained, certainly, by the individual person, but at the same time embracing and shaping the successive multitude of individuals."[1]

The intelligence of wholeness cannot arise when people in the group are locked into their separate-self egos. Nor does it happen at the level of True Self. At the level of separate self, you remain separate from everyone in your community, so you cannot join to create a We Space that will yield a higher wisdom than that which emerges from the collaboration of separate selves. If you are living in True Self, then you are absorbed in the one, and your Unique Voice merges in silence. Collective intelligence is rather a direct function of shared Unique Self experience.

Through the unique contours of your puzzle piece, each member of the group merges with and completes both themselves and the larger whole. The Unique Self experience is both the heart of the phenomenon of collective intelligence and the key to its emergence in any given situation. Said simply, evolutionary We Space is only a genuine possibility if we deploy the awakened technology of Unique Self-realization. There are very few pleasures in life that compare to the awakened We Space of Unique Selves living together. It was toward this pleasure that Teilhard de Chardin pointed when he said, "There is almost a sensual longing for communion with others who have a large vision. The immense fulfillment of the friendship between those engaged in furthering the evolution of consciousness has a quality impossible to describe."

6. To engage in a Unique Self encounter, you must stay open as love through the pain.

To make contact in a Unique Self encounter, you must know how to avoid the ritual of rejection that so often arises from the ego's contraction. When you feel hurt, your small-self ego contracts. Unless you make an effort to counter the ego's inertia, you fall out of divine communion. You fall into *un-love*. Unique Self encounter asks that you not fall out of divine communion and become degraded by *un-love*. It demands that you not get stuck in the coiled contraction of the small self.

The ego will tend to take hurt and turn it into an insult, which offends your existence. Then to compensate, you set into motion the ritual of rejection. It goes something like this:

1. You experience the pain of hurt and/or rejection.

2. As a result, you feel small and insignificant. It even puts you in touch with your nonexistence.

3. To feel less small, you lash out and inflict hurt. In your ability to hurt the other, you experience power, which makes you feel like you exist again.

To enter a Unique Self encounter, you must resist the gravitational pull of un-love. You must identify as part of the larger field of love. This is the source of your authentic power. This will allow you to receive hurt inflicted by others as a wound of love and not as an insult. You wear your hurt as a battle scar in your struggle for love. You bear it with pride and dignity. You are freed from the compulsive need to inflict pain on the one who hurt you in order to prove you exist. You know you exist because you are in divine communion, that is to say, identified with the larger whole beyond your particular part nature. The transcending of ego into Unique Self realization is animated by the quality of love. Love motivates and manifests the spontaneous action of care and compassion. Egoic self-contraction is the quality of fear. Fear motivates and manifests the reactive rituals of egoity.

To live and act as love means to keep your heart open through the pain of heartache and hurt.

To live and act as fear means to allow the pain to close your heart.

You can practice love by practicing opening your heart even when you feel hurt. Rather than turning away, closing down, and striking out, you keep your heart open. This will help you act skillfully instead of reacting clumsily in these situations.

When you practice opening as love moment-to-moment in the face of the hurt, the power of the past weakens. Old wounds are in the past. If you open your heart in the present, time after time, the power of the past recedes.

You will probably always feel the pain when you meet *un-love* in relationship. But you do not need to feel the closure, which deadens your heart and your life force. You can continually practice love rather than closing down into *un-love*. You can feel your self-contraction and choose to change the way you react.

You are not a victim of your past. When you stop either ignoring or overdramatizing past events, you also stop unconsciously using life trauma from the past to avoid giving the depth of love that is yours to give in the present moment.

The pain of the past may have come to you through another. Your present reaction is yours. You are doing it. You must assume responsibility for your own complex of reactivity. Reactive emotion and reenactment do not need to be a fact of your nature. You can take your armor off. You can unguard your heart and trust yourself to live and love from an intense armorless vulnerability. This is the safest place from which to live.

For some people, especially those with fortunate childhood circumstances, opening through hurt is not so hard. For others, it may be the work of a lifetime. For all of us, it is perhaps the most important work we can do for our own love and freedom, and the love and freedom of the others in our lives.

To be weak in love is to exclusively identify with your separate self, which is always already insulted and empty with craving.

To love is to know that we are all lost and found in the same reality together. To love is to stay open in gratitude and joy even as you know that love breaks your heart.

In one of the great mystical moments of Western biblical myth, the patriarch Jacob sees Rachel, the love of his life, for the first time standing by the well. It is the original story of love at first sight. When you see another truly, your seeing plunges you into love. In their first meeting, the story goes, "Jacob kissed Rachel; he then raised his voice and cried."

Why the crying? Answer the Unique Self mystics, "Because he saw he would not be buried with her."

To love is to know that you will feel the pain of separation. This is the paradox of love: love is suffering, yet to live and not to love is madness. We do not liberate ourselves from the suffering of love by detaching ourselves from love itself. Liberation in the path of love is to suffer the mortal circumstances of your love so completely that you are moved beyond yourself. You are moved beyond your small self to your True Self and then to your Unique Self, where you realize that you and your beloved will always meet again. Only then can you love fully from your unguarded heart. You are profoundly in relationship from the fullness of your unique personhood, even as you have evolved beyond the egoic self-contraction of your small self.

7. Unique Self encounters require not only integrity but also evolutionary integrity.

Your Unique Self is also defined by your evolutionary context. In a Unique Self encounter, you seek not only romantic, pragmatic, or emotional connection. You seek evolutionary relationship. In evolutionary relationship, you seek to manifest the evolutionary potential in your meeting. You let go of the narrow narcissistic needs that initially brought you together.

In an evolutionary relationship, you are obligated by evolutionary integrity. You identify the Unique Gift that your meeting holds. You see how this gift supports and furthers the ecstatic, evolutionary God-impulse that motivates and moves all of existence. Evolutionary integrity means that you bring all the people of the past, present, and future who might be affected by your decision into the room. You widen your sense of time from the immediate shallow time to deep evolutionary time.

The ethics of your decisions are then determined not just by the interpersonal matrix between the two of you, but by your evolutionary obligation to all that might be born from your meeting.

CHAPTER ELEVEN

SAY YES

THE CHOICE TO LIVE FROM UNIQUE SELF instead of merely ego is the most fundamental choice a human being ever makes. Every other choice flows from this pivotal point. It is in this moment, which recurs again and again at deeper levels, that you choose to say Yes or No to life. You choose to identify with your Unique Self instead of your ego. This is the miracle of evolution upon which the entire cosmos depends.

Emerson said, "Love is the Universe shouting out a joyful *yes* when our names are called."

In Hebrew the word "yes"—*kein*—means "integrity." Yes is the ultimate affirmation of integrity. The question of your existence is whether you can say Yes to the unique destiny and adventure that is your life. This is self-love! From the place of ego you remain perpetually unsatisfied. Located in Unique Self, everything fills you.

John Lennon tells about the first time he met Yoko Ono. He heard she was having an art show in London:

> So I went and there was a little white ladder that led up to the ceiling. There was a little hanging magnifying glass and something written on the ceiling. So I picked it up and looked through it at the writing. And what was written was "YES." If it had been something like, "rip-off" or something negative I would have left. . . . But it was positive and loving and so I stuck around.

Love is a perception of the infinite specialness, the full uniqueness of the beloved. To love another is to say Yes to their Unique Presence, to their Unique Being and Unique Becoming. The greatest of love affairs begins with a simple imprint of Yes.

Remember, we come into this world trailing clouds of glory with core knowledge of our omnipotence, beauty, infinite power, and infinite potential. And then we hear a chorus of voices for the first ten years of our lives, and the word they most often seem to be saying is No, No, No. We gradually come to associate maturity with saying No. When an idea or new direction comes up, our first response is to posit why it won't work. We are brilliant at it. Even the most simpleminded person becomes a genius when it comes to saying No. We have all become Dr. No with advanced degrees. But somewhere deep inside, the Yes remains, an eternal child of our Unique Self. We know on the inside of the inside that Yes is the answer.

One of the great literary masterpieces of the twentieth century is James Joyce's *Ulysses*. Joyce spends reams of pages portraying the No reality encountered in the streets of Dublin by the main character, Leopold Bloom. Joyce masterfully maps the life of the archetypal human whose life is a series of unnecessary losses: the death of Bloom's son and father, his daughter's leaving, the passing of his youth, and finally the adultery of his wife.

Yet in the last scene of the book, Bloom returns home to his sleeping wife. Never mind it is a recently desecrated bed. Never mind he sleeps with his feet at her head. It is still home, the erotic haven of the inside. The book ends with a crescendo of Yes. As his wife feigns sleeping, we float along in her stream of consciousness, finally concluding with reminiscences of the early ecstatic hours of her and Leopold's love. It is a definitive return to Yes:

> And then I asked him with my eyes to ask again yes and then he asked me would I yes to say yes my mountain flower and first I put my arms around him yes and drew him down to me so he could feel my breasts all perfume yes and his heart was going like mad and yes I said yes I will Yes.

The Yes here is sexual. The sexual in this passage reflects the Eros of life. The overwhelming perfume of this sexual *Yessing* signifies hope, promise, and possibility in the most expanded sense. For the sexual is the full ecstatic urgency of both the urge to merge and the urge to *emerge* throbbing inside of us. This final Yes has magically transformed the seven-hundred-plus pages of modern existentialist No's. It was James Joyce who reminded us that Yes is a feminine word that signifies the end of all resistance.

The high priests entering the holy of holies once a year say Yes with their every step. The cherubs murmur to each other, "Yes, yes." The Temples of God and man are built with Yes stones. The Presence of God is a great green light that says, "Yes, you are gorgeous. Yes, I need you." The Universe is an open entryway, crowned by neon Yes sign. To be lived as love is to know that—as Wallace Stevens reminds us: "After the final No there comes a Yes."

In those heart-opening moments when truth suddenly bursts through your everyday routines, you know that the purpose of your life is to uniquely incarnate the love-intelligence that governs the Universe. Are you willing to utter a sacred "Yes!" to your participation in the evolution of consciousness?

To awaken and say Yes to the unique invitation, delight, and obligation of your life is the reason you were born. It is the only authentic source of joy and meaning in your life. When you slumber and say No, your loneliness, fear, and contraction live in you, through you, and as you. When you awaken and say Yes, you are living as Source. When you awaken and say Yes, Source lives in you, through you, and as you.

The choice is yours, and yours alone. Do you want to live as an isolated ego, deluded into thinking that all you are is your small separate self? Do you want to rely on the limited strength and power of that isolated self?

> Or do you want to open your heart as love, and feel
> all the power,
> all the glory, all the love,
> and all the goodness
> that ever was, is, and will be—
> pouring into you, through you,
> and as you, raising you up and taking you home?

Everything that happens in your life flows from this choice. It is the choice between living disguised as your ego, or taking off the mask and shining as your Unique Self.

When you are merely in your ego, you think you are God's gift to humanity. As a result, you take without asking, and enter without being invited. When you are in Unique Self, you simply are God's gift to humanity.

When you are merely in ego, you pretend that you are God, but deep down you believe that you are not. The gap between your pretension and your belief is the source of all of your pain and pathology. When you are in Unique Self, you no longer have to pretend. You close the gap. You are joyfully living the mystery of your mythology.

Unique Self may be realized by great masters and by the masses alike. There have always been great masters who were able to move beyond their limited personalities and align themselves with the God-impulse. Sometimes they were hidden, and other times they were revealed. Sometimes they were hidden even to themselves.

The evolution of God does not only occur in people who are educated and awake enough to articulate a decision to align with the God-impulse. It occurs every place people say Yes to their highest selves. It is often a hidden Yes, with no audience to applaud. But the Yes is heard in Heaven above and Earth below. All reality claps in ecstatic approval and appreciation.

Some people say Yes because they are expressing their devotion to a God before whom they bow. Others say Yes because they feel God pulsating in their chests as the desire to grow, to love, and to embrace in compassion All-That-Is. Still others, students of Kabbalah, Sufism, Kashmir Shaivism, or contemporary World Spirituality, say Yes because they hear God on hands and knees pleading with them to say Yes. They say Yes with the full consciousness that they are choosing to recognize, in that loving pleading, the evolutionary impulse surging through them as the true reality of their lives.

God accepts all offerings in love.

"Give power to God," writes King David in Psalms. The Kabbalists teach that God is in some insane, paradoxical, and wonderful sense dependent on us. There is a way that God is only as powerful as the power that we give God. We live to be *mosif coach le-maleh*—we "live to empower God," write the old teachers. How? Through realizing the God-spark within you that is your Unique Self, which is God wanting to emerge as you. Through the Unique Gifts that your God-spark obligates you to give.

Are you big enough to be your Unique Self?
Are you a big-enough lover?

Do you have enough guts, courage, and audacity?

All hangs in the balance, and the future of the world depends on your next move. It depends on you.

UNIQUE SELF, WORLD SPIRITUALITY, AND EVOLUTIONARY WE SPACE

YOUR UNIQUE SELF IS RADICALLY SINGULAR, gorgeous, and special in the world. But it is even more than that. Your Unique Self is a puzzle piece that is utterly necessary to complete a much larger puzzle that is vital to our planet today. The unique contours of your puzzle piece allow you to connect with and offer your gift to All-That-Is. Giving your puzzle piece unto the world adds an irreducible dimension to the completeness of the cosmos. Uniqueness is no less than the currency of connection. It is the portal to the larger evolutionary context that needs your service. But it is even more than that. Your Unique Self is evolution waking up as you. Your Unique Self is animated by its puzzle-piece nature. As such, it is naturally connected to a larger context that it uniquely completes. It is paradoxically through the inimitable contours of your Unique Self nature that the alienation of separation is overcome. Unique Self is the source code of all authentic relationships, and it is only through a fraternity and sisterhood of Unique Selves that we can begin to bring profound and loving transformation into the world.

As the great connector, Unique Self is the only technology that can create the evolutionary We Space necessary to affect the evolution of consciousness. Ego cannot form evolutionary We Space. At best, ego can cooperate in limited ways for the greater good. Conscious collaboration, while better than mindless competition, lacks the necessary Eros and imagination to change the world. Unique Self is drenched in Eros and imagination.

One might assume that in order to foster an authentic We Space, we must simply emerge into our True Selves. This is the teaching of the classical enlightenment traditions. Yet we know that True Selves cannot create a We Space, for the total number of True Selves is one. In the grand impersonal realm of True Self, there is only one and not two, and therefore, not relationship and certainly not evolutionary We Space. It is only our Unique Selves that have transcended separateness and entered the larger field of We as unique emanations of the All-That-Is. Enlightened We Space in which individuals and individual systems realize enlightened consciousness beyond ego is the essential technology of transformation for tomorrow.

Unique Self must be fully embodied today, because only through an enlightened consciousness will we find a way to heal suffering and ameliorate needless brutality and pain. Normal consciousness produces suffering. And if you think this is but a spiritual aphorism, then you have only to inquire from the hundred million people brutally tortured and murdered in the last century—all as a direct result of the mad delusions of the grasping ego. The ego of normal consciousness is insane. Enlightenment is simply sanity. In enlightened space, you realize that you are part of the one. You realize that you are not alone, so there is no reason for desperate grasping. You realize that you are not limited to the power, healing, or fulfillment available only to your separate self. Rather, you know that all of the healing, goodness, power, and depth of All-That-Is lives in you, as you, and through you. Not to know this is not to know who you are. It is to be essentially confused about your identity. The confusion between ego and Unique Self is far more substantive than a person simply thinking she is someone else. This is a minor confusion of identity and hence a minor insanity when compared with the sheer madness of mistaking your ego for your Unique Self as your essential identity.

Why is Enlightenment Rejected by Mainstream Society?

Given the power of enlightened consciousness, which I just described, how could it possibly be that mainstream culture, both East and West, has rejected the attainment of enlightenment as the essential human goal? Should not this transformation of consciousness—which can do more than any other force to heal our planet—not be the essential and even passionately yearned-for goal, of both every individual and every collective? Enlightenment is simply not part of the mainstream discourse. Enlightenment is often mocked and at best relegated to the sidelines, not treated as a genuine option for fully normal people. Why not?

The answer is simple, and it is woven into the essential teaching of Unique Self enlightenment. Classical enlightenment says that to attain realization, you must overcome your sense of being special and realize your true identity as part of the one. This instruction is resisted by virtually everyone, for no one wants to give up his specialness. When the price of enlightenment seems to demand that we relinquish our innate sense of being unique and special, enlightenment is rejected by the intelligent mainstream, because at his or her core, virtually everyone in the world feels special. The reigning assumption is that to be special, you must be a separate self, which is the core intuition of the Western enlightenment. So, it emerges that the core intuition of Western enlightenment—that you are separate and therefore special—contradicts the core intuition of the Eastern enlightenment—that you are not separate and therefore not special. As we saw in the main text of this work, for the West, the affirmation of the special separate self is seen as the key to healing suffering, while for the east, overcoming a false sense of separate self and specialness is the key to transcending suffering.

When a person takes their nagging sense of absolute specialness to their spiritual teacher, the usual instruction is to leave behind this feeling of being special, for the desire and experience of specialness is a function of the unenlightened ego. This instruction, while it speaks a great truth, is at its core not fully true. It is true but partial, for it fails to make two essential discernments. Those are the distinctions we have drawn in this work between separateness and uniqueness and between Unique Self and ego. At the level of ego, you are separate, and you are not special. This is the core and correct intuition of Eastern enlightenment. And for this reason, this tradition say you must get over your sense of being a special separate self. But, at the level of Unique Self—beyond your separateness, as a unique expression of the one—you are absolutely and ultimately special. This affirms the dignity of the special individual, which is the core intuition of Western enlightenment. It realizes that you are special, not at the level of separate self ego, but at a much higher level of consciousness, the level of Unique Self.

When you realize your enlightenment, you give up the small games of your ego seeking to reify its specialness, and you move far beyond the alienation of separate self to realize the tremendous joy of uniqueness. You give up the small-self sense of being special as you begin playing an infinitely larger game in the widest context, the game of your Unique Perspective, which has singular gifts to give the world, which can and must be given only by your Unique Self.

The Democratization of Enlightenment

This evolution of the enlightenment teaching paves the way for the democratization of enlightenment. As long as enlightenment seems to demand abandoning the essential specialness of every human being and of every human collective of persons or system of knowing, it will intuitively be rejected by the masses. We all hold an intuition—even if inarticulate—of Unique Self. On a deep level we know that every human being is both part of the great collective consciousness, the creative force of evolutionary Eros that animates and drives All-That-Is, even as she is also a unique incarnation of evolutionary creativity and Eros. Each human being is an irreducible personal expression of the process incarnating infinite dignity and adequacy, as well as being a singular expression of creativity and unique gift. Since every human being is unique, every human being is an irreplaceable and ultimately necessary expression of the enlightened consciousness.

And, it is only through communities built on this We Space, which emerge from the democratization of enlightenment generated by the Unique Self teaching, that we can foster the genuine global commons that is the next necessary and glorious step in our evolution. Spirit awaits our unpacking. This is the evolutionary impulse, manifesting as Spirit in action. Each and every tradition functions as a sort of macro Unique Self, holding a particular medicine that is crucial to the health of the whole. World Spirituality is nothing less than the grand and dynamic gathering of micro and macro Unique Selves who gift the world with their Unique Perspectives and their Unique Gifts, in a way that evolves the one and the whole. It is only through a communion of World Spirituality, in which all gifts from all traditions are taken into account and woven into a higher, integral, evolutionary embrace, that we have the ability to heal our world.

The Why of World Spirituality: Initial Thoughts by Marc Gafni and Ken Wilber

Below are a few preliminary thoughts we would like to share in regard to why evolving the movement we are calling World Spirituality is an urgent need and great adventure of our time. This is not a finished essay; it is rather a set of framing insights that have emerged through our own process of thought and in deep conversation with other leading partners in the movement. All of us are working together closely in catalyzing, articulating, and serving the emergence of an authentic World Spirituality, based on integral principles, that has the potential to provide a context of meaning for hundreds of millions of people.

Let us begin with a bold and audacious statement on behalf of the incredible group of committed leaders from around the world who are coming together to catalyze and incarnate this new movement of spirit. We believe that a World Spirituality speaks compellingly to the hundreds of millions of people who have moved beyond the religions or beyond exclusive identification with any one tradition. And we believe that this may be one of the vital next moves in the evolution of consciousness. Before we go any further, let us state clearly and unequivocally that World Spirituality is emphatically not, in any sense or form, a world religion. World Spirituality is more like a symphony. In the symphony, there are many instruments. Each one is sacred. Each one has its unique music. Each contributes a particular texture and depth of sound to the symphony. But, all of the instruments are playing music. No single instrument can claim to be the music itself. Each one bows before the lord of music. Each instrument plays a unique and gorgeous sound.

World Spirituality engages all the instruments of knowing, including the ancient traditions of premodernity, as well as modern and postmodern wisdom streams. The term "ancient tradition," here, refers primarily to the great systems of religion and philosophy. "Modern tradition," refers, for example, to neuroscience or to the various schools of psychology. And "postmodern tradition" refers to the insights of deconstructionist writers, phenomenologists, ethnographers, and more. Each great tradition has insights that are gifts to the world.

That said, each one overreaches in its claim that its particular insight is the whole story. When the part pretends to be a whole, it needs to be rightly critiqued for its overreach. World Spirituality seeks to be in dialogue with all of the great traditions and articulate a framework in which all of the traditions have an honored place at the table and can benefit from the insights of each other, woven together in a higher integral embrace. The job of World Spirituality is to try to cogently articulate a big picture in which a person might locate him or herself in a larger context of meaning and purpose.

The Who of World Spirituality

Many people at the leading edge of culture and creativity today, who are born in the postmodern world, unconsciously assimilate critiques of the great religious traditions. As a result, religion and sometimes Spirit itself never become a genuine option in their lives. If citizens of the world today carry the wish to engage Spirit, they often meander along, trying to find their way. They are confused and unable to orient themselves to a genuine worldview of meaning that compels, delights, and infuses their everyday life with meaning and direction.

World Spirituality speaks equally to the hundreds of millions of these leading-edge cultural creatives around the world who feel that they cannot locate themselves in a tradition at all, as well as to those firmly ensconced in a tradition who might feel that their identity and hunger is not exhausted by that tradition. They experience themselves as dual citizens—deeply involved in their tradition but at the same time part of the broader global community of Spirit.

One of the key goals of a World Spirituality is to help seekers, all Unique Selves in the world, feel as though they have some direction and guidance on the way, which helps them to identify: What are the issues that need addressing? What are the general forms or types of practice that need to be engaged in order to live on the spiritual path of life? In a sense, the job of a World Spirituality framework is to help people cultivate discernment as they seek to find their way, grounded in Spirit on a genuine path of obligation and freedom.

New Conditions that Catalyze the Evolution of World Spirituality

There are seven conditions that make World Spirituality both possible and necessary today in a way never seen before in history:

1. Global challenges require a global response.

For the first time in history, the core challenges to survival that we face are not local to a particular religion, country, or region. They are global challenges, ranging from the very real threats to the ground we walk on and the air we breathe, to world hunger, to the danger of nuclear weapons falling into the hands of a rogue state, to the most pressing issues of social and economic justice. There is no place left to hide in the word, and the old spiritual truths of the essential oneness of everything, the interconnectivity of it all, is no longer a hidden teaching, but an obvious truth for all to see.

2. Whenever new life conditions come to pass, an evolutionary leap in consciousness and culture is required to meet them.

The global challenges we face require the evolution of a new spiritual collective intelligence, which has the erotic imagination necessary to chart the paths that are essential for the next stage in our evolution. In a time when the threats are world threats, the spirituality must be World Spirituality. The world is in turmoil on virtually every level of reality, even as it is pregnant with possibility and promise. The world faces world problems. Gone is the era when local kings, seers, and shamans dealt with their local issues. There are no more exclusively local issues. Everything affects everything else. Everything is interconnected and interdependent.

Of course, from a spiritual perspective, viewed through the eye of the heart and the eye of the Spirit, this was always the case. However, the essential interconnectedness of all of reality was not apparent. The King of Burma had no felt sense or evidence that his actions and decision would affect the ancient Indians who populated the Americas. Now, however, the underlying wholeness of all of reality, the inextricable interpenetration of all of its parts, is becoming visible to the naked eye. One needs to look only at environmental and ecological issues to realize the essential wholeness, interconnectivity, and indivisibility of it all.

New world conditions are always precisely what necessitate the next evolutionary leap. As we realize that the challenges that confront us are world challenges, we realize that we must evolve World Spirituality to meet those challenges. But not only to meet those challenges...

3. World Spirituality is not just a solution to problems; it is also the delighted expression of the evolving Eros of consciousness, realizing its potential to dance in the dialectical tension between unity and diversity. We are unique and autonomous as people and faith systems. We are also one in communion and even union with each other. Both are true. Autonomy and communion, diversity and plurality, the one and the many dances in higher integration as World Spirituality begins to emerge.

4. We desperately need to recover memory. Not only the memory of the past, but the memory of the future. Without that, there is little hope for the healing and transformation that our individual and collective consciousness so urgently needs. And what is hope but a memory of the future? What exactly is it that we need to remember? Said simply, we need to remember and recover the story. Postmodernity was built on the rejection of any grand narrative. Metaphysics of any kind were deemed the enemy. Any sense of a canon, a worldview, or big picture was reviled and rejected as a violation of postmodern integrity. Paradoxically, however, the grand narrative of postmodernity became that there is no grand narrative. All contexts of meaning that could in any sense guide or even obligate were undermined.

World Spirituality accepts in part the rejection of metaphysics and grand narratives. It recognizes and affirms that core intuition of postmodernity that contexts matter enormously and that no knowledge exists independently of its context. It is furthermore clear to all of us that the grand stories of metaphysics, each claiming to hold exclusive truth, which were virtually all hijacked by various religions of both the spiritual and secular variety as tools of domination, need to be re-constructed for the sake of the evolution of love. World Spirituality based on integral principles is a reconstructive project. No longer can we allow dominating grand narratives to crush the subject, the personal, and the intimate.

And yet, all of that does not mean there is no story. All of the not knowing does not mean that we do not know. All of the metaphysical uncertainty does not mean that there is not post-metaphysical certainty. Nor can we allow for the deconstruction of spirit and what Lewis Mumford called "the disqualification of the universe" and its reduction to become an insipid flatland. Even as we bow before the mystery of unknowing and recognize the post-metaphysical evolving nature of our gnosis, we need to "story up" and reclaim our worldview. We need to once again begin to engage in meta-theory and big picture thinking. For, truth be told, there is much that we know in every discipline. We do have deep knowledge, which has been arrived at through carefully engaging double-blind experiments, enacted in the realms of both the physical and spiritual sciences. We do have shared depth structures of knowledge and meaning, which have been arrived at independently and virtually unanimously by the leading researchers of mind, heart, body, and spirit. We have—for the first time in history—been able to gather their data and reveal the profound shared depth structures of knowledge. These sturdy knowings form the basis of a powerfully effective and inspired human user manual. And when we string together these solid beads of knowledge, a truly stunning integral worldview begins to emerge. This is the worldview of a World Spirituality.

But, in the mad rush to deconstruct all knowing, we have forgotten. We have forgotten that we know. What's more, we have forgotten that we have forgotten. To become whole we need to recover the memory of what we know.

It is precisely a prescient sense of this situation that moved W. B. Yeats to write these famous lines in his poem, "The Second coming":

> *Mere anarchy is loosed upon the world,*
> *The blood-dimmed tide is loosed, and everywhere*
> *The ceremony of innocence is drowned;*
> *The best lack all conviction, while the worst*
> *Are full of passionate intensity.*
> *Surely some revelation is at hand; Surely the Second*
> *coming is at hand.*

The deconstructions of meaning motivated initially by the desire to liberate the human spirit from the shackles of tyranny have run amok and cut the roots of the great universe story that is the Eros and ethos of the All-That-Is sacred and All-That-Is meaningful. So a World Spirituality must be bold, audacious, and rigorous as it weaves together the deepest structures of shared meaning upon which to base the story that we will pass on to our children. It is utterly necessary to re-story and re-enchant the universe in order to create a context for life that is the absolute birthright of billions of people around the globe who have been cut adrift by overzealous waves of deconstruction that sought to de-story the universe.

5. For the first time in history, there is a critical mass of people who have reached worldcentric consciousness. These people have expanded their circle of caring and concern beyond their ethnocentric affiliations. They are at home in the world and feel responsible for the world as a whole, not merely for their country or religion. They cannot be served by ethnocentric religion. For the first time in history, there are hundreds of millions of well-educated people who, although they cannot find their homes in the traditional religions, are searching for a compelling universal set of spiritual principles by which they can live their lives. This can only be addressed by a World Spirituality.

6. For the first time in history, the notion of what we are calling a dual citizen of Spirit is readily understood and available. Not only can one be a dual citizen of two countries, but also, one can remain committed to one's native or chosen spiritual tradition, while at the same time being a citizen of World Spirituality.

7. For the first time in history, the most profound teachings, as well as living teachers from all the great systems of Spirit, are readily available in non-coercive and open-hearted forms. These are available not only to people of that particular religion, but to all who would come to study and practice.

World Spirituality Transcends and Includes the Perennial Philosophy

The perennial philosophy fully revealed itself in the latter half of the twentieth century when great researchers of spirit realized that all the great traditions shared a common set of depth structures. This was not to suggest that there was not real and substantive divergence between the world views of the great traditions but rather to point out that beneath the diversity there is an underlying set of powerful shared truths. The great mistake of the perennial philosophy is that—influenced by the great traditions—it made a premodern move that undermined its own relevancy. The perennnialists by and large ignored or rejected evolution. They located themselves outside of the evolutionary context and consequently tried to reify a set of eternal truths. They did not realize that we have a shared set of evolving truths and in their overreaching claim they ignored some of the key advances of modernity and postmodernity and undermined the cogency and effectiveness of their own otherwise powerful insights.

World Spirituality = Perennial Philosophy in an evolutionary context, with all that this implies. But let us at least make some key points on this utterly essential issue.

It might be fairly stated as follows: to suggest that World Spirituality consists of the perennial philosophy, that is to say of the shared truths of the great traditions, is to be almost certain that World Spirituality will be rejected as an evolutionary emergent. And this is so for two very different reasons:

1. First, if this is what World Spirituality is, the traditions themselves will roundly reject it. If the prerequisite for an emergent World Spirituality is the abandonment of the traditions in the form of reducing their distinctions to a set of common shared truths, then the traditions themselves will be the fiercest opponents of World Spirituality. Again, for two reasons: First, no one likes to be put out of business. Second and more profoundly, the greatness of the traditions often lies in each religion's Unique Self and perspective—which yields its unique insight and practice—and not in the common truths it shares with the other great religions. Often, as I noted above, the perennialist writers and the interfaith proponents of religious perennialism posit as their essential distinction the difference between the depth structures and surface structures of a religion. The argument goes somewhat as follows: The religions differ only in their surface structures, which are determined by the contextual factors of culture and language. Surface structures might include rituals, laws, and specific forms of worship. Underneath, however, are said to be depth structures, which the religions share in common. Depth structures might include the core world-view of the religion, as well as its ethical and mystical core.

This argument is absolutely true, but partial. There are highly important depth structures that are shared in common to some significant extent, both by the mystical and ethical strains of virtually every great religion. This is true. And the gathering of the shared depth structures of the religions was one of the great spiritual projects of the latter half of the twentieth century. Writers such as Fritz School, and those influenced by him, including Aldous Huxley, William Stoddard, Gerard Heard, and

Huston Smith, put forth the core shared tenets of the perennial philosophy of religions. However—and this is a huge however—the differences between the religions are not only rooted in the surface structures of the religions. It is more accurate to say that the religions contain surface structures, on the one hand, and two distinct forms of depth structures, on the other hand. There are, for sure, the depth structures that are shared by all the religions to which the perennials correctly pointed. However, there are also the depth structures that are singular and distinctly rooted in the deepest strata of unique revelation and contemplative insight that nourish and sustain the tradition. The distinction between these insights might be termed the Unique Self of every religion. Unique Self = True Self, which is enlightened consciousness, + Perspective, which is the irreducibly unique perspective of every significant culture.

Buddhism, for example, made huge contributions in understanding and training mind states. Talmudic Judaism made a huge contribution to ethics and social activism in the form of Tikkun Olam, the responsibility to heal and repair the world, based on the infinite dignity of every Unique Self. Christianity made a huge contribution to the evolution and propagation of the biblical teachings on forgiveness.

While each of these traditions dealt with significant depth in all of these three areas, it is fair to say that each of these religions was also specialized, with a highly evolved and unique area of excellence. Each great tradition has its own radically unique worldview, its own distinct medicine, and its own radically wondrous particular contribution to the music of spirit. It would be precisely accurate to say that each tradition is an instrument in the symphony of spirit. It is not only true that all the instruments produce music—much like all the religions intuit and enact spirit— it is also true that each instrument produces utterly unique music—just as each religion enacts utterly distinct forms of spiritual expression. It would be not only ignorance of the most base kind, but tragic, to reduce all the traditions to their shared truths. And, the key opponents of this reductive dishonoring of the religions would be none other than the religions themselves. This cannot be the goal of an evolutionary World Spirituality.

2. To make the common truths of the great traditions the exclusive or even primary content of World Spirituality would be a monumental mistake for a second reason as well. It is absolutely true that the distinction between the surface structures of the religion and the shared

depth structures of every tradition is a crucial insight in the evolution of consciousness and a key part of World Spirituality. This by itself, however, is woefully insufficient as the core of World Spirituality. For, essentially, what that would mean is that World Spirituality is the shared truths of the premodern traditions. In this reading, World Spirituality itself would be a regressive movement. It would be regressive because it would suggest that we be guided by a spirituality rooted in the common insights of the premodern traditions.

That would take us back before modernity and before premodernity, which is exactly where we do not want to go.

Now, do not misunderstand this point. The premodern traditions of Buddhism, Christianity, Judaism, Hinduism, and other great religions, are wildly deep on many levels. The premodern traditions are radically profound at a level of interior understanding, which is most likely beyond anything we know today in our interior reaches. The radical inner focus on Spirit in the premodern age—some would say, the receptivity to the graces of revelation—yielded a depth of interior vision and knowing which is virtually beyond imagination. At the same time, the mainstream of all these traditions remained premodern in many essential ways. They were ethnocentric, marginalized the feminine in various ways, lacked historical consciousness, showed a profound disparity between the elite and the common person, had an underdeveloped sense of human rights, and much more. Each system at its core thought that its truth was primary, if not exclusive, and that in time history would validate its truth claim as the only authentic one. It is precisely that form of premodern religion that is once again spreading around the globe with disastrous results, as evidenced in the meteoric rise of fundamentalism the world over. So, to develop a World Spirituality which shares the best of the premodern traditions—while an evolutionary step in the right direction—is certainly not the final goal of an emergent and evolving World Spirituality.

Rather, as we have already insisted, we want a World Spirituality that shares the best of premodern, modern, and postmodern insights. That would be an enormous leap in the evolution of consciousness. Let's bring on board in World Spirituality the deepest insights of all the great traditions, including all of the great modern and postmodern traditions. This would include the best insights of psychology and psychoanalysis, not least of which would recognize and actively engage what Freud called the unconscious and Jung called the shadow. It would also include fantastic advances in family systems, economics, law, the healing arts, negotiation theory, and conflict resolution as well as the best insights of systems and chaos theory. It would naturally embrace all of the best insights of modern science. It would include critical advances in health care, forms of governance, and human rights. It would include the leading-edge understandings in the postmodern disciplines of hermeneutics, phenomenology, metrics, and developmental thought. This understanding of World Spirituality as embracing the best of premodern and postmodern traditions brings online the evolutionary emergent of Unique Self as a core element in a new World Spirituality.

The How of World Spirituality

At this point, it is essential to locate Unique Self in the larger global context in which it lives. Stated simply, Unique Self is the lodestone of an emergent World Spirituality. World Spirituality has five essential practices, all of which are fulfilled in the awakened realization of Unique Self enlightenment.[1]

Showing up: Unique Self

The core practice of World Spirituality is the Unique Self awakening or enlightenment of every individual. This democratization of enlightenment, in turn, fosters the evolutionary We Space of collective intelligence and creativity, which is essential for the healing and transformation of our world. This is the next necessary step in the evolution of consciousness, which is the evolution of love, which is the evolution of God. This core practice, which animates all other forms of practice, in the terminology of World Spirituality is called showing up. To show up as your Unique Self and give your unique gifts is to awaken as evolution, as the personal face of the evolutionary process.

Waking up: States of Consciousness and Unique Self Waking up has three distinct levels.

1. To wake up means to move from separate self to True Self.

To wake up is to awaken to your true nature, to know that you are not merely a skin-encapsulated ego, but that you are essence. Waking up is the continual movement from ego to essence. In waking up, you realize your true identity; you are an indivisible strand of the seamless coat of the universe.

2. Yet full awakening does not end with True Self. In postmodernity, we realize that everything, including enlightenment, has a perspective. As the last vestiges of sleep are wiped from your eyes, you drop into the realization that you are not only essence, but also the personal face of essence. In other words, you realize that True Self always sees through a unique set of eyes. You awaken to the knowing that enlightenment always has perspective: your Perspective. To wake up therefore means to awaken to the full realization of your unique True Self.

Waking up means waking up to your true nature—not as separate, but a part of All-That-Is. Moreover, you are an infinitely unique expression of All-That-Is. You wake up as the personal face of essence, whose heart is a unique expression of the infinity of intimacy that is the heart of the cosmos. This democratic realization transcends and includes all of the traditions. It is an essential shared practice of World Spirituality.

3. Finally, to wake up is to wake up to the process itself. To wake up means to wake up to the evolutionary context in which you live and to the evolutionary imperative that lives in you, as you, and through you.

In the old enlightenment, to wake up means to wake up to your eternal true nature. As consciousness evolved we realized that your true nature has perspective and it is always ascending and evolving. Therefore, in the new enlightenment, to wake up means to wake up to your evolutionary Unique Self. You are the Unique Perspective of evolution. When you wake up, then the process of evolution becomes for the first time aware of itself. And this is the momentous leap in consciousness that potentially changes everything.

Growing up: levels of Consciousness and Unique Self

To grow up means to up-level your consciousness. Your level of consciousness is the set of implicit organizing principles that create your worldview. These ascending levels or structures of consciousness have been mapped by extensive cross-cultural research done by leading ego developmental scientists over the past fifty years. For example, it has been shown that human beings in healthy development evolve from egocentric to ethnocentric to *worldcentric* to *cosmocentric* consciousness. Each level expands your felt sense of love and empathy to wider circles of caring. In the first level, your caring and concern is limited to you and your immediate circle. In the second level, ethnocentric, your identity expands to a felt sense of empathy and connection with your larger communal context. In the third level, *worldcentric*, your identity shifts to a felt empathy with all living humanity. In the fourth level, you move beyond merely identifying with humanity and experience a felt sense of responsibility and empathy for all sentient beings throughout time, backward and forward. You identify with the process itself and with the unique evolutionary imperative that incarnates as you. This last evolution of consciousness has also been described as the move from first-tier to second-tier consciousness. One of the key findings of developmental research is that as you up-level to ever-higher stages of second-tier consciousness, your unique Perspective becomes readily available. Said simply, according to leading developmental theorists, the more you grow up, the more your Unique Self comes online.

Lighten Up: Shadow and Unique Self

Cleaning up is simply a catch phrase for shadow work, which is an essential component of any integral World Spirituality. The full recognition of the necessity for formal and ongoing shadow work is a modern and postmodern realization, which is implicit but not fully developed in the great traditions. It was Freud and Jung and their respective students who first made shadow work an essential dimension of full human development and health. Unique Self teaching significantly evolves the meaning of shadow work. Shadow is finally realized to be a Unique Self distortion. Shadow is a function of gifts ungiven and life unlived. To clean up is to identify your Unique Shadow and follow it back to your Unique Self, to your unique frequency of light. It is only in light of this Unique Self understanding that it makes sense to actually integrate your shadow, for you are integrating your own displaced Unique Self. This is the essential World Spirituality process of cleaning up, which we call Shadow integration.

Opening Up: Unique Self and Love

Opening up means opening up to and incarnating love. From the perspective of Unique Self teaching, love has three essential components. Love is at its base not an emotion, but a Unique Self perception. To love is to recognize other. The lover has eyes to see the personal essence of the beloved, so love is a Unique Self perception. More than that, love is a Unique Self perception-identification process. To love is not only to perceive the uniquely beautiful essence of the beloved, but to identify him or her with that essence. Second, to love is to stay open through the pain. To love is to open up to the full depth of life, despite hurt, which seduces us to close and contract. You can only stay open as your Unique Self. The ego can never stay open under attack. The third principle of opening up recognizes to love is to give. To love is to be committed to suspending your ego and giving deeply to another for the sake of their higher good, whatever that may be. Once again, you can only truly give to another and stop using him or her to support your existence after you have evolved beyond identification with your ego and realized your Unique Self.

Showing up: Unique Self and unique gift

It is the matrix of waking up, growing up, cleaning up, and opening up that allows you to show up as your Unique Self. It is your Unique Self that gives birth to unique gift. As mentioned earlier in the book, your unique gifts are what enable you to address a unique need that needs to be filled. The core realization of a World Spirituality is that every human being is both part of the whole, and at the same time, a high priest or priestess in a religion of one. The core obligation, joy, and responsibility of your Unique Self is to give your unique gift, fulfilling a unique need in the cosmos that can be met by you and you alone.

Each one of these pillar principles has its own set of practices. In our book on World Spirituality (Marc Gafni and Ken Wilber), and in our World Spirituality Practice Book (Marc Gafni and Tom Goddard), we will outline a complete set of practice modules and guidelines.

World Spirituality is Not the Shared Truth of Premodern Religions

As we have already alluded to, it is not only to the premodern religions that we turn to create World Spirituality. Each great system of knowing—premodern, modern, and postmodern—participates in the forging of World Spirituality. The emergence of modernity with science, the evolution of the social sphere expressed in the rise of democracy and human rights, and the ascension of the feminine are all key components in the formation of a World Spirituality. Can you imagine today a serious World Spirituality without taking into account the implications of neuroscience, what I call neuro-dharma, on our understandings of ritual and spiritual practice? Can you imagine today a World Spirituality without the emergent insights of postmodernity, without its manifestation as multiculturalism and pluralism, without its profound understanding of the distinction between surface structures and depth structures and the role of interpretation and hermeneutics in creating all forms of spiritual and social culture?

Particularly, can you imagine World Spirituality without the evolutions that have taken place in our understanding of evolution? More important than anything, can you imagine a World Spirituality without a profound embrace of the evolutionary context which depends on us and within which we live? The evolutionary context—the realization that consciousness is evolving and that every generation is responsible for giving its own unique gift to this process—is the animating Eros in our attempt to give voice and language to the emergence of a World Spirituality that is already happening worldwide.

World Spirituality is Not Interfaith

World Spirituality is not interfaith. It is a major step beyond interfaith that transcends and includes the evolutionary strides that have been made and are still being made by that great movement of spirit. If one were to map the stages of spirit's evolution from the premodern religions to the contemporary emergence of a World Spirituality in which we are participating, they might be something like the following:

1. In the first stage, when the classical religions reigned supreme in the age before the Western Enlightenment, each religion believed that it was supreme, or at the very least superior, to all the other religions. Much was beautiful and noble and civilizing in these great traditions. And yet their sense of ethnocentric superiority fostered significant shadow. This superiority created in its wake a sense of entitlement, the rationalization for massive oppression, and more often than not, a license to kill. This stage of religious development has been called mythic religion.

2. The second stage emerged with the advent of modernity.

Modernity came along and appropriately weakened the authority of the mythic religions by demanding evidence. Moreover, modernity pointed out that many of the propositions which religions had held to be dogmatic truths were, in fact, factually wrong. These ranged from the view of the universe which placed the earth at the center of all things that the church held as dogma (and was later falsified by Galileo's telescope), to a dogmatically held belief regarding the structure of the human body (which was falsified by the dissections and autopsies of renaissance science), to the belief in the divine right of kings (which was undermined by the rise of the Western enlightenment). Mythic conceptions of religion substantively were weakened. Secularization began its creeping annexations of the world mind. Within the old mythic religions, three distinct progressive voices emerged. First there were those voices often sought to remake the religions in the image of modernity, and generally lost their authentic mooring in the core lineage mind of the religion. Second, there were those who both opened to modernity and maintained a strong and authentic connection to their core religion without formally working out the contradiction between the two commitments. This stage in the development of spirit has been called rational religion. Third, there was in every tradition, a leading integral edge of "dual citizens" who remained deeply grounded in the authentic lineage, even as they embraced an evolving set of modern and postmodern ideas. They were able to discern between the evolving depth structures of their religion, which were good, true and beautiful and the surface structures, which often invited reinterpretation. This hermeneutic process of reinterpretation was seen, however, not as foreign to the religion, but as integral expression of the spiritual impulse itself.

3. The third stage is perhaps characterized by the interfaith movement and has been called pluralistic religion. The interfaith movement made a beautiful contribution to spirit's evolution by getting people talking to each other from the different faith traditions. This movement itself has four distinct expressions. In one expression, what I will call the humanistic expression, the implicit assumption is that the religions cannot be genuinely reconciled at a deep theological level, but if people could just get along at a human level beyond doctrinal difference, this itself would create a mutuality of respect and recognition which would serve to deepen love and lessen religious conflict of all forms. This version of interfaith has been called by contemporary activist and theologian, Charles Randall Paul, religious diplomacy. In this approach, serious "contestation" between religions is encouraged, even as each "contestant" opens his or her heart to "influence," which is a corollary of face-to-face dialogue.

In a second expression of interfaith, what I will call the shared truth or perennial expression, the core issues that separated the religions mattered less because the leaders of interfaith dialogues did not truly take the unique teachings of each of the great traditions, including their own, seriously. In this version of interfaith, the Unique Self of the traditions was often effaced and reduced to some very banal expressions of liberal spirit. Someone once said that the early interfaith dialogues were between Jews who did not believe in Judaism and Christians who did not believe in Christianity, who got together and discovered they had a lot in common. However, this search for shared understanding in the interfaith movement had a third and more profound expression as well. The crucial developmental insight in this third approach was that the shared truths in all the religions are their essential teaching. The shared truth in this version of interfaith both overrides and undercuts what are seen to be the far less important doctrinal, theological, and value distinctions between the religions. This understanding made a highly significant contribution to the realization that what we have in common is far greater than that which divides us.

The core matrices of this highly intelligent and profound interfaith work are the key insights of perennial philosophy. The Perennialists, led by the like of Frithjof Schuon and his circle of students and championed effectively and eloquently by Huston Smith, pointed to the essential shared depth structures, which existed in all the traditions. They distinguished between the surface structures, which were held to be culturally and otherwise contextually determined and the depth structure, which was held to be the shared essence of all religions. And let it be said clearly, the Perennnialist camp and its highly critical insights have made a pivotal contribution toward the evolution of consciousness. And let it be said clearly, the perennial insights are an important part of the emergent World Spirituality. However, let it be understood no less clearly that the shared perennial truths found in all or most of the great religions are only the first step in the emergence of World Spirituality. Perennial philosophy is a part, but in no way the whole, of World Spirituality.

The Evolutionary Emergence of Unique Self and World Spirituality

Unique Self, as we have said, is an essential lodestone of World Spirituality. Like World Spirituality, Unique Self is an evolutionary emergent, which transcends and includes all that comes before it. If you have read this book carefully, you realize that Unique Self emerges from an integration of a number of distinct streams of knowing. Unique Self transcends any particular lineage tradition, even as it is uniquely anticipated in key lineage and cultural traditions that preceded it. Unique Self emerges from the deepest insights of preclassical, premodern enlightenment teaching. Unique Self emerges from modern ideas of individuality, the rights of man and the democratization of power, and a growing awareness of the centrality of evolutionary ideas in all realms of thought. Unique Self emerges as well from the postmodern notions of context, evolutionary context, and unique Perspective—all essential components in the post-metaphysical ontology of meaning-making.

The personal life project of Unique Self invites and obligates every individual in the name of spirit to live their unique Story and give their unique gifts for the sake of the all. It is an ultimate expression of spirit, which cuts across lineage and cultural lines. Unique Self offers a simple yet profound shared spiritual language of World Spirituality that is both accessible and compelling. It addresses the deepest yearning of the human being: to live a life that matters. World Spirituality of this kind is urgently needed today to heal the fragmentation that lies at the very core of the world's heart. It is only this kind of leading-edge evolutionary emergent that will have a wide enough embrace to catalyze a shared world commons. It is only from the space of the shared world commons that we can write a new source code of human culture, rooted in ever-higher levels of mutuality, recognition, union, and embrace. It is only such a World Spirituality rooted in such a source code that will be powerful enough to catalyze this urgently vital evolution of love. It is only through the evolution of love, which is the evolution of consciousness, which is the evolution of God that we will be able to inspire and write a new cosmic scroll. In writing this scroll, we gather as Unique Selves to create an evolving great story that will provide a framework of meaning, obligation, and joy for hundreds of millions of people who are currently cast adrift on the seas of relativism and deconstruction of all world views and big pictures. It is only a new cosmic scroll that will provide us a glimpse at the pattern that connects and makes meaning of our lives, inviting us to higher joy and responsibility. It is only in a new cosmic scroll that all the great religions and all the great systems of knowing and doing will have a place and will therefore no longer seek to usurp the place of another. It is only in the context of such a cosmic Scroll that every Unique Self will have a dignified, honored, and beloved place on earth. And it is only the democratization of enlightenment as the core teaching of that new scroll, written by a congregation of Unique Selves in an emergent World Spirituality, that will send ripples of healing presence and peace across the globe.

AFTERWORD
BY KEN WILBER

WE LIVE IN EXTRAORDINARY TIMES. In the history of all humanity, there have been only five or six major world transformations: somewhere around a half million years ago, humans began to emerge as a distinct species, with an archaic worldview that separated us from the great apes. Around fifty thousand years ago, the archaic worldview gave way to a magical worldview, anchored in foraging, hunting, and gathering. Then, around ten thousand years ago, farming was discovered—simple farming, with a handheld hoe, called horticulture. Concurrently, the worldview of simple magic gave way to mythic-magic—more complex, and more sophisticated.

Around 4,000 BCE, the animal-drawn plow was invented, and horticultural gave way to agrarian, while mythic-magic gave way to fully developed mythic, with its traditional fundamentalistic values. The mythic world ruled until right around the renaissance in the West, when myth began to give way to reason, which exploded during the enlightenment. The rational worldview, along with its scientific materialism, and with its modern values, became in many ways the official worldview of the modern West. Until, that is, the 1960s, which saw the last major world transformation—this time from modern to postmodern, from monolithic reason to postmodern pluralism and the "cultural creatives."

And so, there are the major transformations of humankind—archaic to magic to mythic to rational to postmodern, correlative with technoeconomic modes going from foraging to horticultural to agrarian to industrial to informational. And there the world stood, with its five major transformations—which are, in general outline, repeated today in the growth and development of every newborn individual. Born with an archaic worldview, each individual develops infantile magic from one to three years, mythic-magic from three to six, mythic from six to eleven, rational from eleven onward, with the possibility of post-rational beginning in late adolescence.

The thing about each of these levels of consciousness, which altogether are called first-tier, is that each of them believes that its view of the world and its values are the only ones that are true and real. The mythic fundamentalist view, the basis of most of the world's exoteric religions, believes its truth is eternal truth—the one and only. Rational science, on the other hand, finds myth to be just that—a myth—and replaces it with evidence based truths, which religious myth maintains cannot capture the truly important questions of life (Who am I? What's the meaning of life? And so on), and is an approach for which religion condemns science. And then postmodern pluralism comes along and deconstructs both of them, maintaining they are both nothing but social fabrications with no more truth than poetry or fiction. But this postmodern truth, of course, is maintained to be really real. And so goes the battle between first-tier levels in these endless culture wars.

Sometime during the middle of the twentieth century, pioneering developmentalists began to detect hints of an entirely new and higher level of development—a new and higher level of consciousness. Called integral-aperspectival by Jean Gebser, and integrated by Jane Loevinger, it represented what Clare Graves called "a monumental leap in meaning." Abraham Maslow noticed that it was a move from deficiency motivation—needs driven by a lack of something—to being motivation—needs driven by a fullness, an abundance, an overflowing. Spiral dynamics called this new integral level "second-tier," in contrast to all the previous "first-tier" levels of development. And the difference between first-tier and second-tier? Of course, first-tier levels are all driven by deficiency needs, and second-tier by being needs—but beyond that, where each first-tier level thinks its views and its values are the only real ones, the new integral level realized that all previous levels have some significance, some importance, and therefore are to be included in any truly integral, comprehensive worldview. Where first-tier levels spend their time trying to exclude each other, second-tier spends its time including all of them. As such, integral is the first level historically to overcome partialness, fragmentation, and discord. This is the truly monumental leap spotted by these pioneering developmentalists.

The good news is that studies show this integral level is now, at the beginning of the third millennium AD, starting to emerge in a serious fashion. Right now, approximately 3–4 percent of the population is at second-tier, compared to around 25 percent at postmodern pluralistic, 40 percent at modern-scientific, and 30 percent at traditional fundamentalist. But this 3–4 percent is rapidly increasing, and might reach 10 percent within a decade. At 10 percent, an important tipping point is reached. And with the tipping point, the level's values have profound repercussions throughout the entire society.

In the meantime, those at integral second-tier are already starting to rewrite culture—turning medicine into integral medicine, education into integral education, politics into integral politics, and spirituality into integral spirituality.

Which brings us to the essence of this book, *Your Unique Self.* Before continuing, let me first give you some of the context for the evolution of these teachings within the Integral context. These teachings have been evolved primarily by Marc Gafni for over three decades, drawing from his own realization, insight, and the enlightenment lineage in which he stands. In Gafni's reading of this lineage, brilliantly articulated in his three-volume opus *Radical Kabbalah: The Enlightenment Teaching of Unique Self, Nondual Humanism and the Wisdom of Solomon,* which I read in several highly excited nights, Unique Self is a post-egoic nondual realization of Unique Perspective, which expresses itself both as the Unique Perspective on a text and as the Unique Perspective of the realized individual, what Gafni terms, in Lainer's thought, the Judah archetype, whose perspective is a unique incarnation of unmediated divinity. In essence, the realized individual whose True Self has been disclosed expresses that True Self through their Unique Perspective, what Gafni calls Unique Self. Hence, one might say that the nondual humanism of Unique Self is rooted in the equation I present below:

True Self + Perspective = Unique Self

This teaching was further clarified and evolved in a series of pivotal conversations between Marc and myself in 2005.

These conversations were coupled with intensive dialogue with other leading Integral Spiritual teachers, including initially Diane Hamilton in a catalytic role, and later swami Sally Kempton, as well as important input from Brother David Steindl-rast, Father Thomas

Keating, Patrick Sweeney, Genpo Roshi, and many, many others. All of this took place in a wonderful translineage context provided by the Integral Spiritual Center, which has now evolved into the Center For Integral Wisdom, where Marc and I are partnering with some seventy-five other teachers around the world in evolving a World Spirituality based on Integral principles.

The full crystallization of this New Enlightenment teaching in which Marc and I have partnered and this highly significant new chapter in Integral Theory appear in this radically exciting, groundbreaking book. So with that context in mind, let me continue the story.

Traditional contemplative spirituality—not traditional religion, which involves the mythic level and its literal-dogmatic beliefs, but direct spiritual experience—involves not the evolutionary levels of consciousness, but what are known as natural states of consciousness. Not archaic, magic, mythic, rational, pluralistic, and integral; but waking, dreaming, deep sleep, *turiya* (or the True Self), and *turiyatita* (or nondual oneness), which are the five natural states of consciousness found in all humans according to the world's great contemplative traditions. The aim of traditional meditation is to experience all five states in full awareness, moving wakefulness from gross waking to subtle dreaming, to causal deep sleep, to One Self *turiya*, to nondual oneness or *turiyatita*.

In Integral Spirituality all of those states are still important, and the aim is still to contact and resurrect all five—especially including an experience of one True Self and nondual Suchness. But these direct experiences are now experienced and interpreted not from first-tier partialness, but from second-tier fullness—from an integral level. And so all the traditional contemplative concepts and experiences are reinterpreted from an integral perspective. Not mythic, not rational, not pluralistic, but integral.

And this changes, to some degree, everything.

Take the One Self. Traditionally, the experience of the fourth state of consciousness is an experience of the one True Self, or One True Spirit, in all sentient beings. It's a state of pure, clear, timeless, ever-present witnessing—or unqualifiable, infinite Awareness. The sanskrit term for this is *turiya*, which means literally "the fourth," as in the fourth major state of consciousness, after waking, dreaming, and deep sleep. In Zen, this is your "Original Face," the face you had before your parents were born; that is, your timeless, eternal, ever-present, ultimate spirit self. In

Christian mysticism, it is the state of I AMness—the pure I AMness that you are before you are anything else, the I AMness that you are aware of right now as the simple feeling of being.

The overall number of True Selves is but one. The same True Self in you is the True Self present in all sentient beings. But notice something. Let's say five of us are sitting around a table, and all five of us are 100 percent enlightened, 100 percent aware of the True Self. Each of us has transcended the ego—the small self, the finite self, the self-contraction—and is alive as the One True Infinite Spirit Self. But even though we are all equally the One Self, there is at least one thing that is very different for each of us: namely, the angle we are looking at the table from. Each of us has a Unique Perspective on the table—indeed, on the world itself. So the One True Self is actually taking on a different perspective in each of us. Each of us has a different view of the world, even though each of us is the One True Self. And that means each of us has not just a One True Self, but an infinitely Unique Self as well.

Paradoxically, we each experience not only a singular True Self, which is the same in all of us, but also a radically unique manifestation of that self, special and unique to each of us. Each of us has different talents, different gifts, and different unique views—and enlightenment involves discovering and honoring our differences just as much as our sameness.

After the egoic self-contraction is removed, and after I discover that One Self, that One Spirit, that one reality, how do I manifest it? What special and unique perspectives do I bring to the picture? In other words, how do I discover that my One True Self is actually an infinite, all-pervading Unique Self? How do I honor my Unique Self, discover my Unique Self, manifest my Unique Self?

Well, those are just the questions this book is designed to answer. The Unique Self gets its primary injunction from the emergence in recent times of the understanding of perspectives—the cruciality of perspectives as being ontologically prior (to reality). What the world is composed of is perspectives, before anything else. We say, for example, that the world is composed of holons—wholes that are parts of other wholes. And that's true, but that's already a third-person perspective of what the world is composed of. So it doesn't negate holons; it's just that even that view is a perspective—namely a third-person perspective. There are first- and second-person perspectives of what the world is composed of as well, and all three of those have validity. But that conception itself is something that has only recently been understood.

Prior to this, in both the East and the West, in premodern and up to modern times, the fundamental nature of perspective simply wasn't understood. Things were assumed to simply be seen, because that's the way they are. The world is pre-given, either in the relative way or as eternal ideas in the mind of God, and we are tapping into those and seeing those pure essences. So in the previous understanding, there's a metaphysical foundation to the world that doesn't change, that is true for all eternity, and the only thing that changes is our degree of understanding of these archetypes. The more we understand these eternal ideas, the closer we get to them, and the more enlightened we become. In that system, in the East and the West, the enlightened nature of human consciousness is understood to be tapping into a "True Self"—a real self, a higher self.

There are always two selves in a human being: a small, relative, finite "old Adam" (the egoic self-contraction) and a true, infinite "new Adam" (the One True Self). And with these two selves, the small one is responsible for basically everything that's bad, uncomfortable, unpleasant, and painful, because it doesn't see its connection to these eternal ideas, or these eternal patterns in the mind of God. Awakening to the True Self is the alleviation of that, and by definition, there is only one of those selves.

In all sentient beings, the overall number of True Selves is one.

Now, with the new Integral understanding, there is still a degree of truth to this. As Erwin Schrödinger, founder of modern quantum mechanics, put it: "Consciousness is a singular, the plural of which is unknown."

The overall number of I AMnesses is but one. So every single one of us in this world has direct and immediate access to that One Self—an infinite self that is ever present. Right now that One Self is in some sense hearing everything that's being said, seeing everything that's being seen, knowing everything that is arising. We all have access to that True Self, and our degree of enlightenment is measured by how close we feel to this One Self, how aware we are of this infinite openness, infinite radiance, infinite transparency, infinite unqualifiability.

But even though there's only one True Self in this world, even if every single one of us were to awaken to it, right now, even if everyone shared this absolutely identical sense of One Self, there would still be something that is irrefutably different in each of us. That is, every single one of us is looking at the world from a different angle.

There is only one True Self, but in each of us it has a different perspective on the world.

There is only One True Self, but it is manifesting in as many perspectives as there are sentient beings.

The formula is:

One True Self + Perspective = Unique Self

So my Unique Self is this One True Self, but as seen through the perspective that my body-mind alone inhabits, it is therefore radically unique. So say there is light shining right now, there will be what my gross body sees, what my subtle body sees, what my causal body sees—and even if we are all looking at the same object, we each have a completely different perspective.

And so understanding this formula—One True Self plus Perspective equals Unique Self—suddenly lights up all the individuality of the individual organism that had previously gotten wiped out on the way to discovering the One True Self.

In that journey, following the previous understanding of just One Self, everything is deconstructed and everything is dis-identified with: I am not this; I am not that. Thoughts are arising; I have thoughts; I am not those thoughts. Feelings are arising; I have feelings; I am not those feelings. Emotions are arising; I have emotions; I am not those emotions. *Neti, Neti*—"not this, not that" in this pure emptiness, this pure unqualifiable awareness, this one absolute True Self.

All the multiple intelligences are deconstructed—those are not what I am either. So then in a traditional sense, you end up with your One True Self liberated, but not much idea as to what to actually do with it. How is my awareness in any way different from the *bodhisattva* sitting next to me?

What we really see is that the *bodhisattva* next to me, and next to you, has the same True Self but a different Unique Self—and that Unique Self reinhabits the perspectives that were, in some sense, denied on the way to transcending the ego. That is, the True Self, once discovered and expressed as Unique Self, reinhabits those natural capacities of the human body-mind and all its multiple intelligences. It embraces its capacity for math, or for music, or for introspection, or for interpersonal connection—all the talents and capacities that are given to human beings. These are now reanimated—not from a separate-self sense, but from a True Self, from a radically One Self, One Spirit condition, expressed through your particular perspective.

And that's what makes it unique. That's what makes the activities you then engage in unique. And so this uniqueness is indeed a new version of the traditional union of emptiness and form, because it is one with the unqualifiable vast emptiness that is the Ground of All Being, and that is one with all form that is arising—but now there is an extra little factor added into that. And this is that the awareness of this form is unique in every sentient being. Every sentient being has a unique and special perception and perspective on what is arising.

So that becomes the basis of your particular, special, enlightened capacities. It is the way you can become a true *bodhisattva*—but a *bodhisattva* that is unique to your own perspectives. It is a way to enhance your own talents, and to find your own gifts. And these gifts and talents and capacities are the way that the One Spirit, the One Self, actually expresses itself in the world of form and makes itself known. It's still, in a classical sense, Spirit making itself known—but now it's making itself known through the specialness and uniqueness of each and every sentient being that comes to awaken to the One True Self.

So now there's a whole different way to look at not only what *bodhisattvas* are doing, but how they are doing it, and the capacities they can use, and also to see what really happens in the contemplative process when the Unique Perspective of an individual is realized, and the teaching stops interpreting that as egoic, and we finally end the confusion that Gafni has pointed out; the conflation of uniqueness and separateness.

So there becomes a point in contemplation, once you've deconstructed the ego over and over, and you've gone through causal and gone through *Turiya* and gotten into *Turiyatita*, when all of a sudden in this vast emptiness you are one with everything that's arising, and you feel that oneness and you will still feel a Unique Perspective on how this arises in your experience.

That feeling of uniqueness would traditionally be interpreted as an egoic holdover, which will prevent you from acting in the world on that uniqueness. All that really does is gum up action completely, because the actual number of things that are recommended without a particular perspective on reality are pretty small and pretty bland. These are often stated as common phrases that everyone is supposed to understand: "Love your neighbor," "Don't be selfish," "Don't get attached," "Act with selfless service," and so on, instead of:

Now rest in these perspectives that are arising in yourself, and see how those are inhabited by the One True Self in a way that is unique to you, in a perspective that only you inhabit.

So now it's all about how to spit shine that Unique Perspective, instead of just deconstructing and deconstructing and deconstructing and trying to get rid of any sense of uniqueness—because that's what happens when you're driving toward a pure emptiness without an understanding of inherent perspectival differences. Uniqueness is confused with ego, and denied altogether, instead of being understood as the base through which infinite reality shines.

The capacity for this sort of perspectival understanding is not something that was for the most part completely obvious two thousand years ago, but was oppressed or repressed or not understood by the traditions. It was simply an understanding that evolution had not yet gotten rich enough to bring forth. It was understood that there was *Turiya*, or the One True Self, the Pure Witness, and there was *Turiyatita*, the Witness one with all form, in a true nondual Suchness. But the perspectival nature of all this was not a part of that equation. And as I said, the understanding of perspectives and how they are ontologically prior to anything that arises in the manifest world is itself a recent emergent of evolution. It's something relatively new, coming into existence with the integral level of development. It is One Spirit's own evolutionary realization about itself, which is: not only do I as pure Spirit see the world, I see it through many, many, many different perspectives—all of which are I AMness seeing what is arising, but each being unique and special to the pair of eyes that is seeing the world. And yet I am rich enough to be all of it.

It's a bringing forth, an enactment, an evolutionary unfolding that is itself, in a sense, a harbinger of the integral age. It's an understanding on the spiritual plane or in the spiritual intelligence, concomitant with the type of integral understandings that are occurring in other disciplines as well. And all of these have to do with the emergence of integral second-tier, which is unique because, again, it involves perspectives— and understanding for the first time that all previous perspectives have some role to play in evolution. Whereas in all the thousands and tens of thousands of years that first-tier values dominated human behavior, all we did was try to deny each other's perspective. We could see these perspectives, but we couldn't see through them, and we couldn't take the role of these other perspectives. We couldn't inhabit them. Only by the time we reached the pluralistic level was there enough perspectival power required to make the momentous leap to second-tier.

All these previous perspectives are important, and we have to start including them all in order to really encompass reality. And when we add the infinite dimension to that (namely spirituality), it means that Spirit itself, the One True Self, is realizing for the first time that it can manifest and embody in all these different perspectives, and not just force all of them to be reduced to the perspective of the One True Self. There's still just one True Self, One Spirit, one I AMness—but now all of these involve perspectives that I am taking. And it's the same I AMness arising in all of these perspectives that makes them real. And when a sentient being awakens to who it really is, then they have awakened to their own True Self, which will then show up in them as their Unique Self—because it is their awareness of who I AM as seen through their particular perspective.

I AM is now the sum total of all these perspectives. These are all part of what I AM, even though I will act through my own Unique Self.

And so *turiyatita*—nondual Spirit—is itself evolving. It has evolved to a new level of emergence, which is not just One Self one with form, but oneself seen through many selves, all one with the world of form. And so there's a type of reverse *e pluribus unum* arising: out of One, Many.

The great thing about Spirit's evolution is that it transcends and includes. So we see the essential truths of *turiyatita*; we see the essential truths of One Self, One World, and the union of emptiness and form. All of these are still true. It's just that every evolutionary unfolding adds a new truth—and this one adds the truth that all that previous stuff is still partially true, just seen through various perspectives now. So *Turiyatita is ex uno, plures*—and that, in a sense, changes everything.

There's still the slow evolutionary unfolding and settling in of this new emergent, and so we're seeing the role of integral perspectives settling in across the board of humanity. Maybe 3–4% of humanity is itself actually at second-tier, as we noted, and in the same way we're seeing the switch from the old (but still foundational) form of *turiyatita* to the new perspectival form—evolutionary and unique. That's also a process just slowly taking its role and having its impact in many, many areas.

But the point with these emergents, including the Unique Self, is that they have emerged now in enough people, and in enough minds, and in enough hearts, that they are available to every human being out there. They've become a cosmic habit, a cosmic groove, that is now set. And so it is there, and that's why we can draw on it now, anytime we want. Any sentient being can draw upon their Unique Self, and not just go to the One Self and stay there. So that changes entirely the way that they can relate to their lives—to their spiritual lives, to their *bodhisattva* lives.

As a *bodhisattva*, you vow to go out and change the world. But what are you going to change it with, if not your unique talents and gifts? So even thinking about what you do now as a *bodhisattva* is radically changed by the fact that you're going to act on your Unique Enlightened Self. Your Unique Enlightened Self is going to be the doorway that is going to show you what to do—a new doorway from which you will act, and not just, "I will act on One Self, and my One Self will be the same as your One Self, and we will go out and do One Self things together." That's no way to change the world.

The One Self is still there, but as soon as you come into the realm of manifestation, as soon as you come out of the radical unmanifest, you hit perspectives—that is why there is, for example, an understanding of hitting first-person, second-person, and third-person perspectives of Spirit.

What are those? First person is the person speaking, so that's "I" or "me." Second person is the person being spoken to, "you" or "thou." Third person is the person or thing being spoken about, "him," "her," or "it." And Spirit can be, and has been, approached through all three of these perspectives, whether realized or not. For example, in third-person objective terms, Spirit is a great Web of life, the sum total of the manifest world as a single, great, living, dynamically interwoven system. When you sit on the edge of the Grand Canyon and behold its splendor, you are perceiving Spirit in the third person. Spirit in second person is a great "Thou," a great "other," which is the source and ground of the entire world. Having conversations with God is approaching God in its second-person form. Virtually all the theistic traditions rest on this form. And Spirit in first person is your own True Self, your own I AMness, the One Self in and through all sentient beings.

All three of these forms are true—first person, second person, third person. Spirit manifests in all three of these perspectives, and an Integral view includes them all. And so the first-person degree of spirituality is no longer just I AMness, but unique I AMness, I AMness in its Unique Perspective. And then that infinite true Unique Self drenches and permeates the entire relative system, the entire relative self, and all of its multiple intelligences are drenched in, soaked in, and open to being part of the manifestation of their Unique Self. So that means that it is the combination of this One True Self, one radical Spirit, manifesting through the talents that happen to be awakened in every human being in the particular way that they show and experience their natural intelligences. For some people, the Unique Self will especially show up in emotional intelligence. For some people, it will show up in cognitive intelligence. Some people will be plugged into infinity in their physiological intelligence. Others will find their connection to infinity in other ways, through any of the patterns and capacities and intelligences that are there.

And then, of course, that's when spiritual practice becomes open—both on the way up to discovering the Unique Self, and on the way down to having it manifest—to a lot of practices that can be done to help clarify the Unique Self: for example, clearing up shadow elements that inhibit this realization. Wherever there is growth of any sort, there is a possible shadow connected with it. There is a functional and dysfunctional developmental scheme in everything, and the same thing goes for this new evolution of Unique Self. There's a shadow going with it, too. And so working with shadow takes on even more importance.

There are different forms of practice available now as well. In particular, certain errors are not compounded that previous schools would have made. The previous schools, one way or another, tried to deny any division at all, and let any uniqueness still be vilified as egoic. All that does is get you using contemplation to not only transcend the ego, but to continue denying your Unique Self. And so contemplation becomes a really sticky, messy thing of using your Unique Self to deny your Unique Self. If I wanted to think of a definition of a dysfunctional thing, that's it.

Now, when this existence of absolutely, inherently Unique Perspective is understood, then with that we can go back and still use many of the great practices of the traditions, because many of them are still dealing with parts of reality that have been transcended and included. But we're also looking for new practices. Just like in psychotherapy we're looking for integral psychotherapy, and in medicine we're looking for integral medicine, and in education we're looking for integral education, and in contemplative studies we're looking for integral contemplative studies. We're looking for an integral spirituality that combines a double fullness: the finite fullness of second-tier integral, with its superabundance motivation, and the infinite fullness of *turiyatita*, nondual oneness, now as Unique Self. Not a double lack, but a double fullness, abundance, overflowing.

And that's an entirely new lineage—a trans-path path. This includes all the good stuff of the previous paths, but adds this whole new level of emergence.

And that is something that is extraordinary, and historic, and not to be denied.

SPECIAL DIALOGUE

John Mackey, Co-CEO of Whole Foods, and Marc Gafni on The Unique Self of Business

Michael Ellsberg's interview with John Mackey and Marc Gafni, originally appeared on Forbes.com.

John Mackey, the co-CEO of Whole Foods, is the author (with Raj Sisodia) of *Conscious Capitalism: Liberating the Heroic Spirit of Business of Capitalism.* Philosopher Marc Gafni, Ph.D., president of the Center for Integral Wisdom, is the author of *Your Unique Self: The Radical Path to Personal Enlightenment.* Michael Ellsberg is the author of *The Education of Millionaires* (find more of his writing at *Ellsberg.com).*

While these are very different books, the authors have been in dialogue for years now about interesting crossovers in their thinking. In this dialogue, we captured some of the new ideas the two thinkers are pioneering for the future of business, centering around their concept of "The Unique Self Business."

Michael Ellsberg: One of the things that was clear to me reading *Conscious Capitalism* was the focus on systems. That was the theme that just kept leaping off the page, and what was different in your perspective than that of the average manager. Instead of analyzing each component separately with separate metrics, you have a strong emphasis on seeing the entire system, within the business, but also beyond the business: how the business relates to all of society and the environment. Would you agree that systems thinking is a central theme of the book?

John Mackey: It's definitely one of the central themes. The stakeholder approach to business sees integration rather than separation, and sees how things fit together. Analytical intelligence—the type of intelligence that it taught in school, which carves things up into little pieces to understand them—is crucial. But it is limited. I use the metaphor of a cadaver in medical school. They carve it all up, so you understand how things divide up into parts, and you gain a great deal of understanding that way. But remember, it's a dead cadaver—it's not alive. The 100 trillion cells that make up that body are not living any longer, they're not interacting. Studying a cadaver won't tell you very much about wellness.

Similarly, the way most people approach business—and the way they mostly teach in business school—involves the analytical mind. It divides it up and looks at parts in isolation. In contrast, in our work, we're trying to show how everything fits together in the larger system. You have to manage the system. Most good leaders intuitively know this, they're just not conscious of it. They understand that they've got to take care of their customers. They get that their employees can't take care of the customers well if their employees aren't flourishing. And they get that they need to treat their suppliers well, which provide them everything they don't produce themselves.

Most managers get this. The next step we took was to see how these all fit together. Once you begin to grasp that they're all interdependent, then you begin to grasp that the best strategy would be to optimize the system. That was a Eureka moment for me—many years ago when I grasped this, I got up and ran around the house and figured it out. "Oh my God, you've got to manage all of these things together. You've got to try to optimize the whole system!" I still think that it's a revolutionary idea.

First, I could hardly believe it. Surely there must be trade-offs, right? That's generally the criticism you hear about the stakeholder model. The analytical mind usually thinks in terms of tradeoffs. So the thinking goes, if you're doing things for the customers, then maybe it's not good for the shareholders. If you're helping one person, someone else must be losing. Zero-sum.

The idea that in the system, if you manage it in an optimum way, all of the constituent parts of the system also win, flourish, and benefit, is intrinsic to business and even to capitalism itself, properly understood. But people don't understand it because we're not taught to think that way. If we're not taught to think that way, we don't see it.

Ellsberg: Why do you think so many managers have trouble seeing this way? It seems like an obvious point yet as you say, it's actually a revolutionary idea in the business world.

Mackey: I puzzle about this a lot. I would have long conversations with people and they just couldn't get it. They couldn't get past the analytical mind. What I concluded was, systems thinking takes hard work. It doesn't come naturally, it doesn't automatically happen. It's something that you have to develop. You have to work on it, you have to practice it. To learn the violin, you can't just pick up and play; you've got to practice it. In the same way, you've got to practice systems thinking. Until you do, this won't make sense.

When you talk to people about the stakeholder model, you get some people saying, "This is so ridiculous, this will never work, this is such BS, this guy must be some New Age hippie." And then they see that I'm very successful, and so it calms them little bit. Then other people think, "Duh, this is so obvious, I don't know why we even bother to state it, it's a tautology." It's interesting that you get people that think it's utterly ridiculous, and others that think that it's so obvious that it doesn't need to be stated. It all depends upon whether you have a systems mind. If you have it, you see it automatically. You can't explain how things work in a system to somebody who can't see it. They're blind to it, they can't see it.

Ellsberg: One of the problems is that it's very difficult, if not impossible, to develop metrics relevant to complex interactions of interdependent systems. The whole analytical model is based on simple cause and effect.

Mackey: Yes, the analytical model does not do well with multiple causes and multiple effects and interactions and interdependence, and feedback loops. What you can do is measure each of the stakeholders, in terms of how well they're flourishing or not. Your typical business just measures the metrics that have to do with the profitability of the business one way or another. But you can have metrics that measure employee happiness and the morale. You can also do direct customer surveys, you can track it over time, you can do supplier satisfaction scores as well. I would say that we have barely scratched the surface in terms of the types of the metrics that can be developed relevant to the stakeholder and systems model. I think over time, as stakeholder thinking and the systems mind spreads, I think we'll see lots "metrics entrepreneurs," so to speak, who are creative and come up with ways to measure overall flourishing of the system.

Ellsberg: While metrics are obviously important, in some ways, even the urge to reduce everything to metrics seems like part of the problem. There are certain qualitative things that are very subtle and can't be captured well even on surveys. I mean, imagine if you tried to run a marriage on metrics…

Mackey: I've got good news for you, I've taken a survey and we're doing well! [Laughter] I think that's very true. The analytical mind is saying, if you can't measure it, it's not real. And yet we know that there are things that don't lend themselves well to measurement, but they're still real. It's hard to measure love, but there's hardly anything one could imagine that's more important than love. And yet you can't really measure it. I can feel it. I can know whether a store has got a good energy or whether they're afraid or whether they feel safe—whether they're happy, whether there's a lot of love… I can feel it when I'm in there, but I'd be hard pressed to quantify it.

Ellsberg: Probably the most common criticism of the ideas in *Conscious Capitalism* is that, "This is all so idealistic, but it will never work in the real world. "

Mackey: If that were true, it would be a damning criticism. Because nothing succeeds in business like success. If ideas win in the marketplace, they spread. If they don't win in the marketplace, they tend not to spread. So, the biggest criticism of conscious capitalism by people who are skeptical is, "Yeah, that's great but it won't really make money." It's seen as a philosophy for losers.

But, as I discuss in my book, conscious businesses outperform in terms of higher morale, in terms of better customer satisfaction, in terms of greater supplier loyalty, in terms of their community philanthropy and care, in terms of their environmental impacts. And they outperform economically. That's why I know that conscious capital ideals are going to spread. Because they're going to win the marketplace.

That's one reason why I wanted to talk to millennials. We wrote the book really for millennials. The millennials will create the conscious businesses in the 21st century. They'll transform the world. And we want them to know that they're not being suckers. This actually is a better way of doing business, not only from an ethical standpoint, but also from a financial standpoint. When that word gets out, we're going to have a very rapid transformation.

Ellsberg: Marc, while your book is not explicitly about business, in many ways it covers the same themes as John's book. It's all about the interdependence (rather than opposition) of the individual and the whole.

Marc Gafni: The concept of the separate self, a strong individual identity distinguished from family, clan, tribe, kingdom, emerged in the Renaissance. Interestingly, not long after, it emerged in business. All of the sudden, corporations aren't just extensions of the king, who takes profits and puts them back into the treasury. All of the sudden, the corporation emerges as an individual identity with a life of its own. These two developments changed the entire trajectory of economic emergence.

So, you've got the separate self of the corporation, if you will, and you've got the separate self of the individual. Both are conscious of their uniqueness, but neither is conscious of also being embedded in a system. It's an attitude of, "We're going to survive. We're going to get the best we can." Hobbes's notion of a world of war where everybody's got to claim what they can. It is a zero-sum game. I get more, you get less.

But then as you develop, as you emerge more deeply, and as business emerges more deeply, we begin to realize, "My business is part of this larger system of stakeholders—stakeholders being community, and environment, and their kids, and the next generation and all of the suppliers and all of the customers and all of the employees. I'm part of this large system, and we're all interconnected.

But that realization does not require you to then collapse and lose your individuality into the system. On the contrary, your unique self, as an individual, and the unique self of the business, are part of the system, part of the whole. You begin to realize: "If I wasn't here, it would be a value proposition that wouldn't be offered in the world—my business has a purpose. My life has a unique self. My life has a purpose. There's a unique expression of the creative intelligence of the world that lives uniquely as that business, that's not being expressed and can't be expressed, by anything other than that person or that business. So, the business really is a self. Just like the person's a self, and they're actually very, very parallel.

John really awakened in me a core intuition that was nascent but needed more information to flourish, the inherent goodness of business. I grew up in a liberal culture in which business is demonized. This seemed counter-intuitive. Business, after all, supplied jobs and human dignity to so many people. Upon reflection, it became clear to me that business has actually lifted more people out of poverty than any other force in history. Business has lifted more people out of survival needs and allowed them to evolve their consciousness, allowed them to engage in higher levels of consciousness, higher needs. Business actually feeds families, allows girls to get an education, and creates the context for meaning, in which most people are living today.

However, every business needs to measure itself against the same high standard that every human being does: having a unique purpose, a unique gift to give.

One of the topics of John's book, which moves me greatly, was just the description of several billion people on the planet whose needs aren't being met adequately. When you say, "whose needs aren't being met adequately," that's a nice way of saying that they're starving. 20 million children died of hunger last year, and there are 17 million actual slaves in the world. The world's filled with horror as we sit here.

Where's the solution going to come from? It's not going to come from bureaucratic government. It's going to come from unleashing the unique selves of as many people, and as many businesses with purpose, on the planet as possible. This is where conscious capitalism and unique self begin to cross-pollinate. Each idea needs the other and together something very powerful, creative and good emerges.

Conscious capitalism rooted in the recognition of the infinitely creative unique self of every human being is a critical evolutionary attractor, serving the evolution of the good, the true and the beautiful. One of the shared key realizations that are beginning to emerge from our conversations, is the game-changing concept that a corporation, like an individual, has a unique self. Just like an individual awakens to their unique self so does a corporation.

Just like there are at least two versions of self: the small or egoic contracted self which views itself as separate from the larger contexts, vs. the more awake unique self which experiences itself as the irreducibly unique expression of the seamless coat of the universe. In a direct parallel to ego vs. unique self in the individual, there is the ego vs. the unique self of the corporation.

There is the egoic self of the corporation rooted in what is called the shareholder model, which views itself as a relatively isolated monad seeking its own prosperity, needing to interact with others only for its own interest, vs. the corporation awakened, to its own unique self which sees itself as offering a unique value gift to reality and yet views itself as enmeshed in its larger context. The unique-self corporation operates based on what is called the stakeholder model—of which Whole Foods may be the leading model—in which all of the stakeholders are viewed as interdependent, all part of the larger interconnected whole.

Mackey: Conscious capitalism is the process of waking up individual leaders to their purpose, to their higher purpose within the large systems that they're part of. But, it also aspires to do more than that. It wants to wake the *corporation itself* up. In a sense, there is a self there. Whole Foods Market, for example, has a self. I got this fairly early on because I'm the father, the creator—and it has a destiny apart from me. The saddest thing is when parents get their children to do what they want to do and be perfect reflections of them, and they haven't recognized the unique self of their child. They're narcissists, they see the child as just an extension of themselves.

A lot of entrepreneurs can do that with their corporations. They see it just as an extension of themselves. It is important to understand that you may have been the father or mother, the creator, the entrepreneur, but that it has a unique self.

But most corporations are not awake to their own unique self. They are not awakened to their higher purpose. Why do they exist? The default answer, and this is why corporations are so disliked and distrusted, is that they're profit machines. Or as the documentary *The Corporation* tried to show, they're sociopaths who are basically running around, exploiting people, taking the resources of the world, dumping toxins out, just for their own gain. Like an ego run amok. Instead, corporations have to awake their collective consciousness to their higher purpose.

It reminds me—I remember watching this Star Trek episode a long time ago. They run into some kind of powerful robot spaceship, a nomad, and it's purpose was simply to reproduce itself, and part of what they had to do was get the robot to its consciousness, that it had a higher purpose, it had a higher mission. Well, in a sense, that's what we have to do with corporations, because they have to awaken to their own unique self, their own higher purpose, and their own destiny. My generation hasn't done that. It's a good task, frankly, for your generation. It's a good task to create unique-self conscious businesses. And we have to transform the legacy ones, or get rid of them, because they often behave like sociopaths.

Ellsberg: I think probably whatever resistance that you've gotten to your message, from the liberal side, has been that people see so many of these unconscious businesses that are—as you said—kind of these disconnected egos, polluting rivers, colluding with corrupt third world governments, these kind of things, all in the name of maximizing profit. What is going on there when a company feels that it has no connection to the earth, has no connection to human rights, no connection to anything other than itself. It is just sort of running amok. What's causing that?

Mackey: It's asleep. It just hasn't awakened yet, it's not conscious yet. That's why consciousness is such a good metaphor for it.

I'll tell you an interesting thing that I learned in the book world, about who likes the message and who doesn't like the message. It's very surprising to me. I thought that I would get a lot more pushback from business people. I didn't. I got almost none. When the business people get this message, it's more of an enlightenment, an awakening and it's like "Yes, of course, this makes total sense." I expected that the business people would think that this is soft, this is wimpy. But no, the business people love it. I've been thanked hundreds of times by business people.

Young people also get it. The millennial generation gets this. They grin, they get excited. The people that are resisting this idea are people of my generation, who already have a mental model in which "business is evil, and it's greedy and it's selfish and it's exploitative," and they don't want to give their mental model up. They've invested too much in it. That's why you've heard that saying, "progress in society generally occurs one funeral at a time." I'll say that I've kind of given up on my generation. I think that my generation's got ideological lock-in at this point. The solutions are there, but they don't want them. To have to think and change their worldviews is difficult, and most people that are older don't want to do it. That's why I think that it'll really be the creation of the next generation. I talked about this yesterday when I was down at this conference that Arianna Huffington did. Someone asked, "How can we change the big corporations?" And I said, "We don't have to change them. They're going to die. They're a dinosaur and they're going to go extinct. Some of them will change, but they'll be rare. What will generally happen is you'll have these entrepreneurs create these new businesses, following new models.

How many people were on Google 15 years go? It barely existed 15 years ago. How many people were on Facebook 10 years ago?' It barely existed ten years ago. So, what ends up happening is you create new businesses, and they change everything. That's why it's essential that you begin to create these more awake businesses. There's a parallel with the unique self: conscious business leaders help a conscious business to awaken, but a conscious business helps everyone that interacts with it to awaken. It's a very powerful vehicle for awakening.

Gafni: An evolutionary strange attractor.

When you talk about business it is simply wrong to identify business by its lowest common denominator. How do you identify what humanity is? Do you say "let's take the greatest sages and seers, Buddha and Lao Tse and Moses and the best of people and say that's humanity?' Or should we take the mass murderers of the last hundred years and say "that's humanity." Obviously, what we're going to say is that humanity in it's highest is what humanity truly is. The lower expressions are distortions of humanity rooted in fear, trauma and ignorance. If Plato had one important idea it was that evil is rooted in ignorance. Modern psychology has added trauma and distortion to the list. But humanity as its core is humanity at its best.

So, the conscious capitalism corporations are, on the business side, the expressions of the business self in a way that the seers and great saints were in the individual human self-side. In other words, we basically look to the greatest thinkers, the greatest embodiments and say, "that's the strange attractor." That's what the system's moving towards. And one of the key things that those great saints have done is that they've actually given to the world a vision of what it means to be an awakened human being.

Now let me take this one step deeper. The vision of the great sages and seers of enlightenment was true, but partial. It was accurate, but limited. Because of its limitation, which I will explain in a moment, that vision of enlightened self, suggested by most of the great traditions, has been in large part rejected in contemporary modern and postmodern culture. That is a great loss, because the enlightened vision of self really is a critical strange attractor to call forth the emergence of the evolved human self. The problem is that the part of the vision that does not resonate in contemporary culture is so fundamental that the baby got thrown out with the bath water.

Let me explain. The enlightenment world, so strong in Eastern religion, which is now fairly popular in certain sectors of the cultural creative population in the West, has become irrelevant to the larger mainstream, because the enlightenment world's vision is primarily about awaking to True Self. True Self is the singular that has no plural, the merging of identity with the greater One. Classic Eastern or mystical enlightenment is about realizing you are not a separate self, but rather you are part of the One. Separation is an illusion.

Now watch something super cool unfold here! Paradoxically the word enlightenment is also used in the West—Western enlightenment—but in an opposite way. The Western enlightenment says that you are a separate self; you are not defined by any larger context. This freed the human being from the church and king. The Western key to Western enlightenment is that the source of your dignity is being a separate self independently valid, not dependent for your dignity and value on any larger context.

So there is this huge contradiction between Western and Eastern enlightenment. You have two movements in society calling themselves enlightenment, saying pretty much opposite things. The Western enlightenment says your separate self is the source of your value and dignity and identity, while the source of your suffering is having your identity defined as being inseparable from a larger context. The problem with the Western position is that is true but partial. You are not merely separate. The most subtle and speculative minds in every great tradition—validated poetically by systems theory, chaos theory complexity theory and much more—all affirm that you are not merely separate, you are in you very core identity inseparable from the whole and identified with the whole.

Now get this. The Eastern enlightenment folks say the opposite of the Western folks. They say that your identity as a separate self is the source of your suffering, and your wider identity with the larger context is the source of your liberation. Just the opposite of Western enlightenment. Now the Eastern mystical approach is—no surprise, right—also true but partial. You see you are not merely part of the one, as the East suggests you are, also distinct and individual.

The way to integrate these two great insights is to make an essential distinction in the nature of *distinction itself.* There are two different ways you can be distinct. You can be separate or you can be unique. Both the East and the West lump them together. The East says they are both bad and the source of suffering (separate self and unique self are viewed as synonyms). The West also views them as synonyms, but they are viewed as the course of your value and dignity. Because in the classical Eastern mystical teaching, separateness is identified with uniqueness, uniqueness is thrown overboard. Your uniqueness is thought to be an obstacle you need to overcome. It is a function of your conditioning.

Key to our breakthrough in Unique Self teaching is to correct the conflation and distinguish between separateness from uniqueness. You need to move beyond your separate self to overcome suffering. You realize your identity with your True Self. But then you awaken more deeply and realize you are a unique expression of True Self. Your uniqueness is actually a robust essential identity on which you can build your life, whether that is the unique self of the individual or the unique self of a corporation. That is the great source code evolution of Unique Self. The key is that uniqueness is not a function of my separate ego self, or of what is called conditioning, but rather uniqueness is an expression of essence. This allows us to re-embrace uniqueness as an enlightened expression of essence and not merely as a function of separation and contraction. That opens the door for the unique self and the unique self-corporation as essentially and vital expression of essence and spirit.

Just as the concept of the Unique Self is redefining the structure of what it means to be a human self, the concept of the Unique Self corporation is redefining what it means to be a corporate self. Conscious capitalism is redefining the very ethical basis of business, but it's more than the ethical basis of business. It's redefining what the optimum business looks like. It's fostering a new positive and accurate myth of what business is, which serves as a new evolutionary attractor for the future of business.

Mackey: I totally agree with everything that you said. As we create manifestations in the world of conscious organizations—not just conscious businesses, because it can be… the next book that we're working on is called conscious society. We need conscious governments, we need conscious non-profits, we need conscious organizations. Culture permits people to go higher quicker because the environment that they're in helps lift people up, because the environments that they're in helps lift people up. Of course, the culture, if it's a toxic culture, will hold down the people. That's why it's essential that we have more than this individual enlightenment type of metaphor—you go off and you become enlightened and study under a guru and it's very much mysterious and you do these practices. It's an awfully slow way for humanity to advance.

We're in a period of time right now where the whole planet is under massive stress. Our economy is under stress; we're bankrupting ourselves incredibly rapidly. We're under very intense stress. It's also a great opportunity, because the stress does bring out more creativity and innovation and what not. So, we can't afford to wait for the old paradigm of the individual enlightenment. It's too slow.

That allows for transformation to occur fairly rapidly. It might've taken decades and decades and decades before but I think now it can happen much faster. It'll be because organizations collectively are resonating in this much higher way, and then they help lift not just their employees up, but everybody that interacts with them.

Gafni: Now, let's introduce a new idea. Let's call this new idea by two complimentary names: the democratization of enlightenment and the democratization of creativity. Both enlightenment and creativity used to be for the elite. The elite were the only enlightened and creative ones. The rest of us were just doing our thing. But the concept of unique self suggests that we actually have to democratize enlightenment, meaning that every human being is an awakened unique self. And every corporation can actually awaken to become a conscious capitalism corporation, that is, a corporation enlivened with profound competitive advantage, because it is formed by the radical creativity of all of individuals in the company.

This tracks to exactly what John describes at the end of his conscious capitalism book—the decentralized model of Whole Foods, in which basically you've got this intertextured layer of teams, and all of the teams have a strong level of autonomy. They're trained and empowered with a lot of mastery, and each has its own purpose. Because it's decentralized, everyone feels a sense of autonomy, a sense of power in the best sense of power, and they're able to unleash their creativity. So, Whole Foods has unleashed probably an exponentially larger dimension of creativity than almost any other company around. Now compare this with a company in which only the 30 people in the most senior leadership roles are truly creative. So, all of the sudden, you've got 80,000 people who are creative. So that's democratization of creativity, which is part of the same impetus as the democratization of enlightenment.

Mackey: The reason that corporations haven't wanted to democratize creativity is because they're so terrified of it blowing out of control. There's such a strong desire to control things, so they damper it down, they make rules. But the trick is, you can't simply democratize creativity unless the creativity is naturally guided by the shared core values of the corporation. You don't control it in a sense through command and control, but the higher purpose of the organization is what aligns the energies and the creativity moves towards the unique self of the employees, and the of the corporation.

Ellsberg: This is, I thought, one of the most interesting points in your book. I've never seen it elsewhere. If you ask most CEOs "What's your purpose?" You'll get an answer like, "to maximize shareholder value." It's completely generic and it doesn't actually speak to what they're doing. What you said is, "we start with a clear purpose." It's this paradox that people seem to not be able to get their heads around, or a lot of people can't get their head around. "We start not focusing solely on money, and we'll actually end up making more money, because we're doing something that we care about and we're passionate about."

At one point, I heard you say something like, "we hired our first investors." Now that, to me, is a really interesting viewpoint, because instead of saying, "We'll take whatever money we can get, whatever they think that our business should be, whatever their attitudes are," instead you're saying, "No, this is who we are, and if you want to invest in our business, you need to understand that these are our values, this is our purpose, this is what we're up to, this is how we run things."

How does that work, now, however, being a public company where there are all of these regulations and a fiduciary duty? Does that change it?

Mackey: No, because this is the best strategy to maximize profits and long-term shareholder value. Most of the rest of them are failing at this goal—because they're making shareholder value their most important goal, but they aren't achieving it. They're actually letting shareholders down. The Whole Foods way, paradoxically, results in higher shareholder value. That's the clever way of saying it, but the more accurate way of saying it is that Wall Street is agnostic about purpose. As long as you produce good results, then they tend to think that it's a good idea, and Whole Foods Market has been amazingly successful from almost the very beginning. Conscious business tends to be very successful financially and so Wall Street loves us. This is clearly the trend of the future, as everyone wins.

John Mackey, the co-CEO of Whole Foods, is the author (with Raj Sisodia) of Conscious Capitalism: Liberating the Heroic Spirit of Business of Capitalism. Philosopher Marc Gafni, Ph.D., president of the Center for Integral Wisdom, is the author of Your Unique Self: The Radical Path to Personal Enlightenment.

FOOTNOTES

Chapter 1: The Great Invitation of Your Life

1.　It is worth mentioning that the idea of love as an evolutionary catalyst can be traced to the great American philosopher Charles S. Peirce and his famous essay "Evolutionary Love," [*The Monist* 3 (1893): 176–200]. Peirce offers one of the first and best post-Darwinian evolutionary metaphysics, and his ideas foreshadow much of contemporary complexity, chaos, and dynamic-systems theorizing. But his vision, unlike that of most disciplines, was of a universe with depth, and one moving toward love. He was an important Integral progenitor. (According to Zachary Stein in his article "On the Normative Function of MetaTheoretical Endeavors" [Integral Review 6, no. 2C (July 2010): 5–22], "Peirce [articulated] a broad evolutionary vision of the universe where the strivings of humanity are continuous with the evolution of the cosmos. It was a sophisticated and empirically grounded evolutionary ontology where all events are semiotic processes that co-evolve toward increasing complexity, autonomy, self-awareness, and possible harmony. Peirce's pansemiotic evolutionary theory was a unique [post-metaphysical] view insofar as it was explicitly offered as a hypothesis amenable to correction in light of forthcoming empirical data. It greatly influenced Whitehead and continues to intrigue and inspire scholars in the physical and biological sciences and philosophy.")

This understanding of evolution allowed Peirce to bring his overarching normative concerns about the trajectory of academic discourses in line with a venerable philosophical tradition that articulated the radical significance of humanity's cultural endeavors in terms of a cosmic evolutionary unfolding. Ultimately, Peirce, with a look in Kant's direction, envisioned humanity as capable of multitudinous self-correcting intellectual and ethical endeavors, which ought to result in an ideal communication community coterminous with the cosmos. In this post-metaphysical eschatology, the ideals of harmonious love between all beings and unconditional knowledge about all things stand as goals to be approached asymptotically. With this thought, Peirce rearticulates a philosophical motif that can be traced back through Emerson, Schelling, and Kant to the obscure cipher of Böhme's mystical Protestant religiosity and its ancient Hebraic and Neoplatonic roots.

Evolutionary love is later a major motif in the world of Teilhard de Chardin and in many of the contemporary evolutionary thinkers who write in his wake. Notable among them is the work of Brian Swimme, who writes in the wake of Thomas Berry and who speaks of the allurement that is the very glue of the Universe. The contemporary understanding of love at the cellular level augments the understanding of the great traditions, some of which also saw love as the primary motivating force of the cosmos. This is the primary position of the Kabbalists, such as my lineage teacher Lainer of Izbica, rooted in Luria and in the earlier Zoharic texts, as well as of many Christian thinkers like St. Thomas and Dante, who talks of *l'amor che move il sole e l'altre stele*, the "love that moves the sun and the other stars." For St. Thomas the "dynamic pulse and throb of creation is the love of all things for the infinite" (New York: HarperCollins Paperbacks, *The Forgotten Truth: The Common Vision of the World's Religions*, 1992, p. 78). Spiritual teacher and scholar Sally Kempton points out that in the Hindu text of *Spanda-karikas* and other major texts of the Kashmir Shaivism and other Indian traditions, love is described as the intrinsic motivator of the substance of creation. A text called the *Maharthi Manthari* describes how Shakti, the creative power of the divine, leaping forth in her own bliss, manifests this universe as an expression or even an outpouring of love.

Chapter 2: The New Enlightenment of Unique Self

1. Living "in you, as you, and through you" means that Unique Self is refracted through all the prisms of your consciousness.

An Integral View of Unique Self Overview

Unique Self is a liberating realization that promises to integrate the so-called trans-egoic, No-Self teachings of Eastern traditions with the individuality emphasized in the West and the uniqueness that is inherent to all human beings. We would offer Unique Self as a living koan; an inquiry meant to provoke curiosity, exploration, and presence, rather than an attempt to reify or fix our self-understanding.

We understand that Unique Self can and will be interpreted differently according to personal inclination and constitution, cultural orientation, and differences in stages of development. For example, a Benedictine monk, whose realization validates an eternal transcendent soul, may understand Unique Self as an expression of that unique soul. A Zen Buddhist, whose realization does not posit a reified transcendent, may experience Unique Self as the freedom to manifest exactly as we are: complete, whole, empty, and unique. In another example, a secular materialist might understand Unique Self as an expression of one's unique perspective and abilities to succeed and develop.

In each case, we would hope that the Integral practitioner would see that classical enlightenment, in the formulation of the great traditions as a realized state of unity with the oneness of all ever-present reality, is recognition of what might be called "True Self." This realization finds that the total number of True Selves only and always is one. This, however, is only true in unmanifest oneness. There is no True Self anywhere in the manifest world. At the same time, every person's awakening to this oneness arises through their own Unique Perspective. In this way, True Self plus my own perspective equals my Unique Self.

In developmental-psychology terms, the fullest flowering of Unique Self might best be articulated as a living glimpse into the "Indigo" stage of human consciousness and self-identity: this is the stage of evolution of human consciousness at which my felt ever-present unity of reality—a state of ongoing "flow presence," if you will—and the unique characteristics of my own life and perspective—the unique evolutionary features of my life—clearly intersect and find a cohesive and stabilized integration. At second-tier and third-tier, perspectives are inherent in awareness. It is an inherent aspect of what emerges at Turquoise and Indigo. So even though Unique Self was present from the earlier stages of consciousness, it can seem to emerge at second-tier and third-tier. Perspective is an inherent part of the realization of the Indigo structure. When someone develops to Indigo, they know that they are looking through a particular perspective even as they recognize other perspectives, and are even to some extent able to disidentify from their own. And my own perspective is never absent, even as it is progressively clarified and deepened through the evolution of self to Self. It is important to note, however, that proto-expressions of Unique Self appear in significant ways in earlier stages of consciousness as well.

Our Intent

Our efforts are meant to provide a vibrant, open, and enlivened look into the emerging potential of the possibility for humanity at this stage in our evolution. In the first-person perspective, Unique Self is a practice of recognizing the profundity of your own life, the preciousness of your specific perspective, history, and talents, and the opportunity to become fully who you already are—I am uniquely this. In the second-person perspective, Unique Self is minimally an opportunity to see and support the Uniqueness of others' gifts and to foster a durable community that supports the evolutionary possibilities of humankind—I see who you uniquely are. At a higher level of inter-subjective space the collective intelligence of evolutionary We space becomes possible. This is one of the core features of Unique Self encounters. And in the third-person perspective, Unique Self can be understood as an evolutionary emergent—a subtle, gentle, yet powerful and compelling whisper from the emerging future of humankind—this is who we can become.

The Foundation of Unique Self

World Spirituality based on Integral principles provides a foundational program upon which to reconstruct spiritual insights and human meaning-making in a modern world that has transcended merely literal interpretations of religious mythology and seeks to transcend the nihilistic and narcissistic assertions of atheistic scientism and postmodern relativism. Unique Self rests squarely on the "post-metaphysical" core of Integral World Spirituality.

Tenet 1: Perspective is foundational.

Integral World Spirituality maintains that the deep structure of reality is composed of perspectives. Whether we take this commitment as "strong" (ontologically real) or "weak" (usefully descriptive), we can still easily understand that all sentient creatures have a perspective.

Tenet 2: Uniqueness is obvious.

All human beings and perhaps all sentient beings will have a unique perspective. This perspective will be unique on the one hand due to different location—all perspectives have a unique angle of perception—but also due to the different psychology, biology, culture, and history of each creature and its context. According to the realization of the eye of the spirit, human uniqueness is essential, and that human beings' location reflects the unique dimension of divinity that literally births the individual.

Tenet 3: Perspectives evolve.

Going further, we see that all sentient creatures have their being arise in four quadrants—those of subjective experience, biological, cultural, and social dimensions—and that each of these quadrants is holonic in nature. Therefore, each aspect of reality evolves over time and thus perspectives will also evolve over time.

Tenet 4: "Conventional" metaphysics is unnecessary.

There is no necessary metaphysical aspect to perspectives. At the same time, while a metaphysical perspective is not necessary to an engagement with Unique Self, there is nothing about perspective that precludes ontological revelations. Perspectives thus create a common ground up and down the spiral. In the post-metaphysical view they arise, for example, in human beings and evolve over time, inexorably influenced and co-created by the evolution of all four quadrants. We need not make any necessary reference to any transcendental concepts or extra-evolutionary features to describe Unique Self. At the same time, Unique Self does not exclude communities who hold a set of realizations that they signify as pertaining to the transcendent (e.g., God). Thus every perspective grounded in direct experience supported by a valid community of interpreters has an honored, if partial, place at the Integral table.

Tenet 5: Ego need not be transcended or obliterated.

"Ego" is a term that is used in many ways. We will use "ego" in this context to mean the general patterns of self-understanding and self-identity that developmental psychologists have tested and articulated using Integral's Zone 2 research methodologies (the outside view of an individual-interior reality). Of course, viewed from within our own subjectivity (i.e., Zone 1), these same patterns "look and feel" as purely phenomenological realities. Because this usage of ego is around an enduring line of self-development that extends up and down the first-person holonic spectrum, it is inaccurate to think of ego as being transcended per se. Rather, ego expressions become more inclusive, subtle, refined, and expansive with each successive stage of development and envelopment. When the West first ran into the Eastern traditions, particularly Theravada Buddhism, and first met the whole notion of transcending self, the ego was made bad in all ways. You had two columns. In one column was ego, which was equated with the devil, and in the second column was non-ego, which was equated with God. The critical Western insight of ego being the functional organizing center of conventional awareness, which is utterly essential in the finite world, was effaced. This was a disaster because if you get rid of ego in the finite world, you are borderline or psychotic. You're not enlightened.

Tenet 6: We are never outside of a state, and always within a stage.

All "structure-stages" of consciousness get enacted only within the ontology of present-moment states. We are never outside of the now. So states describe a "substrate of awareness" in which the real arises (and gets interpreted), and stages of consciousness can be understood as the large-scale characterizable patterns of these moment-to-moment interpretations. So we can discuss a state of deep presence, flow states, or nondual identity. But as any uniqueness of self comes into the picture, there will always be a stage particularity to the interpretive act. It makes no sense to talk about Unique Self as a state outside of a particular developmental stage. Unique Self is always interpreted through the prism of stage development.

Tenet 7: Unique Self is fully expressed at an "Indigo" stage of consciousness.

After considering all other tenets above, it is clear that Unique Self therefore can best be described as the stage at which general patterns of ego development evidence an integration between stabilized "No-Self" insight (e.g., cosmic identification) and one's own felt-sense of uniqueness in their life, talents, and history (i.e., their four-quadrant evolution). This stage has been empirically mapped and articulated using Zone 2 methodologies as the "Indigo" self.

We might describe the subtle and refined ego of the Unique Self understanding as one that has let go of the exclusive identification of the subject with its separate self. The transcending of the egoic separate self through repeated access to "presence-flow" states is the goal of classical enlightenment teaching. This, however, does not mean that the ego is annihilated. Rather, the exclusive identification with the egoic separate self is overcome. We are able to experience our fundamental identity—not as an ego isolated from other, nature, community, and All-That-Is—rather, as part of a larger whole. Note the similarities of this description with how researchers have characterized the Indigo stage of ego development:

> [They] experience themselves and others as part of ongoing humanity, embedded in the creative ground, fulfilling "the destiny of evolution" and are in tune with their lives and their shared humanity "as a simultaneous expression of their unique selves." (Susanne R. Cook-Greuter, 2002, http://www.stillpointintegral.com/docs/cook-greuter.pdf)

That is, these individuals are capable of integrating the unity of reality realized only in deep presence-states (the "creative ground") and their own uniqueness as a living expression of a dynamic evolutionary process that continually will call on them for their special contribution ("the destiny of evolution"). We allow for the possibility that glimmerings of this stage of consciousness, where Unique Self has emerged as this integration, can appear up and down the spiral of human development.

A more rudimentary version of the following note was occasioned by a debate between Robb Smith and me from the post-metaphysical nature of Unique Self enlightenment. The original version of this note was coauthored by me, Robb, Diane Hamilton, Ken Wilber, and Sally Kempton. It appeared in the ISE1 attendee guide.

In our discussion of the Indigo level of consciousness, a potential distinction between the premodern realization and postmodern Indigo realization of Unique Self suggests itself. For much of the premodern world (excepting many of the great realizers and their inner circles who founded new schools of thought), Unique Self was a deduction that went something like this: "Since we all view the mountain from a different perspective, we all have a unique perspective." At the postmodern, second-tier, and third-tier consciousness of Indigo, Unique Self is not only a deduction but a realization. Every person at Indigo has direct access to what only the great realizers were able to access in the premodern world.

2. "Seamless but not featureless" originally appears in R. H. Blyth, *Zen and Zen Classics, 5 vols.* (Tokyo: Hokuseido Press, 1970).

3. See Wolinsky, *The Way of the Human: The Quantum Psychology Notebooks* (Capitola, CA: Quantum Institute, 1999).

4. Naturally there can be healthy and unhealthy prisoners in the cave. The West focused on making the prisoner in the cave healthy by clarifying the false self, taking back shadow projections, and so on, in order to have a healthy separate self. The problem with this approach is that the prisoner is still in the cave, which is the source of suffering. The East focused on getting the prisoner out of the cave by moving from separate self to the realization of True Self. The problem with this approach is that the realization of True Self does not heal all the neurosis or pathological dysfunction of separate self. It is only in Unique Self that we embrace both the individual uniqueness of the self, which naturally requires clarification, and at the same time realize the True Nature of the individual as an indivisible part of True Self, the seamless coat of the Universe.

5. Any experience of formless True Self, when it manifests as any object at all, manifests as the Unique Self. So to repeat, there is no True Self anywhere in the manifest world. There is always a perspective—that is to say, True Self always manifests as Unique Self. That means Unique Self is always the source of awareness, "all the way up and all the way down." Of course, Unique Self is always present as the witness of consciousness at all levels of awareness, because awareness or consciousness is always embodied in form, and therefore always has a perspective. Unique Self, however, becomes progressively more conscious and full in direct proportion to one's level of True Self-realization. The base awareness of Unique Self is True Self. True Self is the actual origin of awareness at all levels of development, even though it only comes online as conscious awareness with the stage of enlightenment, or what Integral Theory has referred to as third-tier growth. The point is that there is no True Self in the manifest world. The True Self is always looking through a perspective. So in the manifest world—that is to say, in the only world we know— there is only the Unique Self. Only pure, formless unmanifest awareness is pure perception without a perspective. In this unmanifest state there are no objects, only consciousness without an object, so there is nothing to take a perspective on. This can be said to be unqualifiable True Self. But we live—always—in the world of manifestation. Once the awareness of True Self manifests, it does so through a particular perspective. That is always the Unique Self.

6. With the emergence of second-tier and particularly third-tier structure stages of consciousness, perspectives themselves become noticed. So at this stage the conscious realization of Unique Self fully emerges. It was of course present all along but tended to be confused with True Self because perspectives were not yet fully conscious. But when the full awareness of perspectives emerges, the awareness of Unique Self emerges. Then any experience of formless True Self, when it manifests as any object at all, manifests as the Unique Self.

7. The centrality of perspective was simply not understood in the premodern world the way we understand it in our postmodern context. We used to think we were directly engaging reality as it is. This is why every spiritual system thought that it owned the truth. Every system thought it was seeing reality itself. This was only half true. At some point we began to realize that there is no reality without perspective—or put another way, reality itself is fundamentally constructed from perspectives. There is nothing we see that is not filtered through the prism of perspective. True Self cannot exist independent of your Unique Perspective. Thus, every enlightenment realization is defined in part by the unique perspective of the practitioner.

Of course, perspective itself can be understood from many perspectives. Perspective might imply ontology, methodology, or epistemology. All of these understandings of perspective appear in the old Hebrew texts, which unfold perspective as the central hermeneutic category of textual interpretation, which is the essential spiritual act of the Talmudic homo religiosus.

In the matrix tradition of Unique Self, which is that of Talmud and Kabbalah, taking different perspectives on the sacred text is a central spiritual practice. Judaism is first and foremost a textual tradition. The nature of a textual tradition is that competing readings of the text need to be explained, especially if the text is said to be divine. How can it be, it is asked, that different readers of the text, with different and often mutually exclusive readings, all express the word of God?

This question is answered in a number of ways. Each is based on a different reading of the idea of perspectives. The champions of methodological pluralism claim that in fact only one reading of the text is correct, and the other readings are granted equal status simply because we lack an appropriate method to inform us which reading is correct. In this reading, what is emphasized is the limited nature of each perspective on the one hand, and the hierarchy of perspectives on the other; namely, one perspective is better than the others because it more clearly captures the true intention and meaning of the divine text.

On the far other side of the spectrum are the champions of an ontological pluralism, who assert the radical ontology of perspectives as the core tenet to be recognized and affirmed. This position is rooted in both the classic Hebrew legal and mystical traditions, for whom the text was thought to be a living expression of divinity that did not exist independently of the perspective of its reader. "God, Torah, and Israel are One," is an old Kabbalistic dictum, which essentially means, "Reader, God, and text are One."

In one expression of this teaching, this ontology of perspectives is thought to originate at the source event of revelation, the theophany of Mount Sinai. In this teaching, every person standing at Mount Sinai during the time when the divine voice was heard is said to have stood at a different angle in relation to the mountain. As a result, each person heard a different voice of revelation. And in a nondual matrix of realization, each Unique Perspective on the mountain is understood to have yielded a unique voice of God. This is an ancient version of the New Enlightenment teaching of Unique Perspective, which creates Unique Self. For the Kabbalists who assert ontological pluralism rooted in perspectives, the validity of the hermeneutic is based on the unique perspective of the interpreter who is situated at a unique angle toward—and therefore experiencing and incarnating a unique expression of—the divine face. It is this unique angle that dictates a person's Unique Letter in the cosmic scroll. This original insight of perspectives in regard to revelation becomes the matrix for a sophisticated ontological pluralism in Talmudic and Kabbalistic sources.

Related to this pluralism in regard to the voice of revelation, there emerges what has been called the one-letter teaching of Lurianic Kabbalah. In this teaching, each person is regarded as having their own letter in the Torah. In one-letter theory, your letter in the Torah is both the ontological source and purpose of your existence. Your individual existence is both rooted in, nourished by, and intended to realize your Unique Letter in the Torah scroll. Your Unique Letter is your Unique Self, your Unique song whose notes are formed by your Unique Perspective.

8. This realization of love as the motive force—as the very feeling and glue of the cosmos—is the underlying enlightened realization of Unique Self mystic Isaac Luria and his school. Luria's school includes perhaps the most important, profound, and influential teachers of Western

mysticism, who inform the core teaching of evolutionary spirituality that would later emerge in the writings of the great German idealist Schelling and his colleagues. This mystical insight is slowly finding its way into the leading-edge discourse of science and spirit.

9. This is the second-person expression of evolutionary love in the intersubjective context. In third-person evolutionary love, will appears as the Eros that coheres and persuades the Cosmos toward unfolding.

Chapter 3: Two Visions of Enlightenment

1. It also appears in spiritual liberation traditions like Hinduism and mystical Judaism and Christianity as the communion of the separate self with the divine. Similarly, the Western enlightenment tradition, which affirms the separate self in some versions, affirms the goal of the communion of the separate self with the divine.

2. The mystical understanding of enlightenment, East and West, focuses on what Integral Theory has referred to as *states* of consciousness. Enlightenment is some form of satori, metanoia, redemption, or awakening. It is a state of consciousness that is at once always already present and at the same time requires realization.

In contradistinction, the exoteric Western deployment of the idea and term "enlightenment," the idea that produced democracy and human rights, is referring not to a state but to a *structure stage* of consciousness. By structure stage, we refer to an internalized worldview that represents a particular level of development, for example, magical, mythic, rational, pluralistic, or integral. These levels of consciousness have been extensively described and evolved in the context of developmental and Integral Theory.

The West has pushed into what have been termed by developmentalists orange/rational structure stages of consciousness (Graves, 1974), which express themselves in areas like representational democracy and human rights. The Eastern traditions (and some Western mystical lineages) have pressed into the higher states of awakened consciousness, expressed in different forms of satori, awakening, communion, metanoia, and *unio mystica*. While the West acknowledges states and state stages, they are not part of what might be termed the "official" Western orientation. Unique Self is both a state of consciousness, which like classical mystical enlightenment is available—in a flow state for example—at any level or structure stage of consciousness. Unique Self is also a structure stage of consciousness revealed in and as the expression of the second-tier structure stages of consciousness when perspective is revealed as an essential structure of higher consciousness.

3. In an email correspondence with Ken Wilber, after much conversation at his loft and over the phone in 2005, I formulated the core understanding of Soul Print/Unique Self as perspective, as emergent from Hebrew mystical sources on the ontology of perspectives. In this understanding emerging from Hebrew mysticism and from deep conversations with Ken, including his radical emphasis on perspective, Soul Print/Unique Self was understood as the perspective attained at the post-egoic enlightenment level of consciousness. I have kept my note to Ken in its original form to capture some of the energy and excitement of these early conversations:

Giga Pandit,

So much love to you! In terms of Soul Print/Unique Self, it is very important to understand that soul prints do not emerge from the world of ego or soul but rather from radical nonduality. Soul Prints is an expression of the Self with a capital S. The way I teach it to my students, Story and non-Story are one. Or in the expression of the great vehicle of Buddhism, Emptiness is form and form is emptiness. Or in classic Kabbalistic expression, Keter is Malkhut and Malkhut is Keter. This is what I refer to as "a nondual humanism" in the fullest sense of the word.

To explain what I mean, let me offer a simple map of the three classic levels of transpersonal consciousness that—as you [Ken] have pointed out—show up one way or another in virtually every system. We can call them Communion, Union, and Identity. Communion, which Scholem felt was critical in Hebrew mysticism, is ultimately dual. God in the second person. Union moves toward nonduality, and full nonduality is achieved in Identity. Or we might use the more classic terms, which you deploy in your wonderful essay "The Depths of the Divine"—psychic, subtle, casual, and nondual. Or we might call them Ego, Soul, and Self. Or we might call them *ani, ayin, ani.* Or we might use Eastern terms in which "psychic" and" subtle" might be roughly equivalent to *savikalpa samadhi*. At the highest edge of *savikalpa samadhi*, the way I understand it, there is already a glimpse of the formless void of the next stage.

This next stage of formless union, what for some Kabbalists would be called *ayin*, the realm of the impersonal, approximates the Eastern state of *nirvikalpa samadhi*. This is a stage of formless awareness that is beyond the personal. You call this stage the causal state. The highest and deepest stage is, however, beyond even the formless state of *ayin, nirvikalpa samadhi*; this is the non-dual that is the very Suchness of all being. It is the Suchness of both emptiness and form, both personal and impersonal. This is the world of One Taste or *sahaj* in Eastern terms, or the *shma* declaration of *hashem echad,* "God is one" in Judaic consciousness.

The way to reach the ultimate nondual realization— for example, according to my teacher Mordechai Lainer of Izbica—is through the prism of soul prints or Unique Self. Soul prints is the absolute and radical uniqueness of the individual, which is the expression of emptiness in form; it is *ein sof,* revealing itself in the only face we know—the face of unique form. It is not only that there is absolutely no distinction between the radically personal and the radically impersonal; it is also that in terms of stages of unfolding, the radically personal is the portal to the embrace and identity of the absolute one. Moreover, the absolute one expresses itself only through its infinite faces, or what have been called its infinite soul prints (or Unique Self).

Another way to say this might be to borrow the image suggested by the Midrash in this regard, that of the ascending and descending ladders on Jacob's Ladder. For the Kabbalists, this is the ladder of nonduality. On the ladder are angels of God. "Angel" in biblical Hebrew refers to a divine entity or to a human being. What they share in common is that each is a radically unique messenger of God. Or said differently, each is a radically unique perspective. One ascends to the divine through soul print, and the divine descends through soul print (Unique Self). Indeed, all human reality as we know it is soul print (Unique Self).

But even this language is insufficient. For in the experience of nonduality, soul print (Unique Self) is the divine. So one ascends to the divine through the divine soul print (Unique Self). And divinity descends to the divine world of form through the divine soul print (Unique Self). All faces of divinity are kissing each other. What the sages of old called *nashkei ar'a verakia*, "the kiss of heaven and earth."

Now, another term for soul print might be "perspective." As we have pointed out many times, the classic image for unique form or soul print in Hebrew consciousness is *panim*, face. "Face" is an expression in Talmudic language for what we moderns and postmoderns might call perspective. This is what the ancient sages meant when they taught: "There are seventy faces to Torah." Torah contains objective God-givens and yet can only be read through the prism of perspectives.

Ultimately in Hebrew mysticism, each human being is the bearer of a Unique Face that is by very definition a unique perspective (Unique Self). This is a radically particular perception of the world, which is shared exactly by no other being. In this sense, the person is the eyes of *ein sof*, of the absolute. The person is the eyes of the Absolute in a way shared by no other being on the planet. This is the source of our grandeur, our infinite adequacy and dignity, and occasionally our almost unbearable loneliness, which for this very reason can only be ultimately quenched in the caress of the divine.

How does one get there, to the soul-printed merger with the absolute? In Hebrew mysticism, through erotic merger with the Shekhinah. This might take place through many methods of practice, including the concentrated, intense, and ultimately ecstatic study of sacred text (*Hasidei Ashkenaz*, in the twelfth century, and the Kabbalah of the Vilna Gaon and his school), the intense meditation of sacred chant and song (classic

Hasidic practice), the rigorous and uncompromising process of introspection and dialogue, with results in the clarification-purification of motive and desire called *berur*, out of which the Unique Self naturally emerges (Luria, Izbica, Mussar), classical mystical techniques of letter combination, soul ascent, meditation, crying, and more. Total Love, Total Good!

Mega Reb

My note to Ken, emergent from our many conversations, clarifies both the post-egoic nature of Unique Self—that is to say, Unique Self is fully realized only as an expression of True Self—as well as the identification of Unique Self with Unique Perspective. At Integral Spiritual Experience 2010, both Ken and I gave keynotes on Unique Self in which we crystallized many of our conversations, and for myself, twenty years of writing and thinking in this regard. Ken's wonderful formulation in his keynote was "True Self + Perspective = Unique Self."

It is also critical to note that from an Integral developmental view your perspective on the world is largely informed by your level of consciousness, and indeed it is refracted through the entire prism of AQUAL, all quadrants, levels, line types, and states—the core matrix of Ken Wilber's Integral Theory.

4. Bruce H. Lipton, *The Biology of Belief* (Carlsbad, CA: Hay House, 2011, p. 70).

5. James L. Oschman, *Energy Medicine in Therapeutics and Human Performance* (Edinburgh: Elsevier Limited, 2003, p. 20).

6. In fact, in Hebrew the words for "love" and "obligation"—*chovah* and *chibbah*—are derived from the same root.

7. To be clear, state development, from separate to True Self, is insufficient to heal suffering. We also need structure-stage development, to higher levels of consciousness from mythic rational to pluralistic to second-tier. "Static development" refers to the process of waking up to your True Nature. "Stage-structure development" refers to the process of growing up to higher levels of consciousness, for example, growth from egocentric to ethnocentric to world-centric consciousness.

8. Lest you think we are misreading *A Course in Miracles*, let's look at the highly popular book *A Return To Love* (New York: HarperCollins,

1992), a popularization of the Course in Miracles by Marianne Williamson (p. 110): "From a course perspective special means different (unique), therefore separate, which is characteristic of ego rather than spirit."

Chapter 4: Eight Stations on the Road to Unique Self

1. This teaching which I call the "Three Stations Of Love" is the basis of the Integral Spiritual Experience and will form the core of the forthcoming book, *The Three Stations of Love*. I have used the term "stage" here instead of "stations" in order not to confuse the Three Stations of Love with the Eight Stations of Unique Self. In general, however, I prefer the term "station" so as not to confuse the term "stage" which in Integral Theory refers to Levels of Consciousness.

2. The full recognition of the centrality of shadow comes online only in the modern period. The great traditions had what might be termed a proto-shadow awareness that was profound but not developed.

3. William Blake, *Proverbs from Hell* (New York: Oxford University Press, 1975).

4. In Hebrew mysticism, this vow is taken by the hidden realized masters who are said to participate in the soul/root of the prophet Elijah.

Chapter 5: The Story of Story

1. The sections "The Grace of the Story" and "The Loss of Memory" are a free mixing of my Soul Print teaching and language in part IV of my book *Soul Prints* (New York: Atria, 2002), as well as oral teachings on story that I have been giving since around 1996. Other formulations come from Jean, including the phrase, "A myth is something that never was but is always happening." (I don't recall if that phrase is Jean's or Joseph Campbell's.) I wrote *Soul Prints* in Israel several years before I came across Jean's teaching. When we did our first public dialogue (in Ashland, Oregon, April 2006), we were both struck by our shared passion for story.

2. On the compelling moral context of the evolutionary worldview in both Abraham Kook and Jesuit Teilhard de Chardin, see Hugo Bergman, *Teilhard de Chardin and the Idea of Evolution*, in Abraham Uderachim as cited in Yosef Ben Shlomo, *Poetry of Being: Lectures on the Philosophy of Rabbi Kook* (Mod Books, 1990).

Chapter 6: Ego and Unique Self

1. See A. H. Almaas, *The Pearl Beyond Price* (Boston: Shambala, 2001).

2. To reach enlightenment, you must be able to take a perspective on your story. This is the Hebrew mystical reading of Abraham, who is commanded to leave his land, birthplace, and father's house, that is to say, to step out of his perspective and take a perspective on his perspective. This same teaching is the deeper intent of the Talmudic teaching, "Anyone who says something in the name of the person who said it brings redemption to the world." Let the hint be sufficient to the wise.

3. Humanity emerges from its semi-immersion in the Great Mother. As the human sense of separate self solidifies in what is called by anthropologists "the early farming period," so too does the person's terror of death.

Chapter 8: Joy and Unique Self

1. Talmud, Tractate Shabbot, 30.

2. Talmud, Tractate Sanhedrin, 34 and 47.

3. The original Hebrew word is *hevel*, usually translated as "vanity," as in "vanity of vanities, all is vanity." However, the literal Hebrew word *hevel* means something closer to "insubstantial." It is in this sense that the mist created by our breath on a cold day is called *hevel*. It is with this same sense of the word that I have re-translated Solomon's famous verse as "illusion of " instead of the more standard, illusionary "vanity of vanities."

Chapter 9: The Ten Principles of Unique Self Shadow Work

1. J. Ruth Chandler, *The Book of Qualities* (New York: Harper Paperbacks, 1988).

2. I am not suggesting that Bly actually believes that the baby is the ideal. Rather, Bly is committing the classical pre-trans fallacy typical of many neoromantic thinkers, who confuse pre-personal radiance with transpersonal maturity and realization.

Chapter 10: Evolutionary Intimacy

1. I am indebted to my friend and colleague Craig Hamilton, who gathered these key quotes. See Craig Hamilton, "Come Together: Can We Discover a Depth of Wisdom Far Beyond What Is Available to Individuals Alone?" in the journal, *What Is Enlightenment*, May/June 2004.

Epilogue: Unique Self, Global Spirituality, and Evolutionary We Space

1. The distinction between waking up and growing up was originally published by John Welwood in *Toward a Psychology of Awakening*, (Boston: Shambhala, 2000, p. 231). Mariana Caplan (Boulder, CO: Sounds True, *Eyes Wide Open: Cultivating Discernment on the Spiritual Path*, 2009) points out that Chögyam Trungpa used to have people practice by saying "om mani padme hum,"—grow up. The om mani phrase expresses the enlightened state of consciousness called the Jewel in the Lotus. In effect, Trungpa was saying wake up and grow up. In a conversation with John (2011), I suggested that Trungpa, who was his teacher, was the inspiration for his core distinction between wake up and grow up, which John readily acknowledged. Trungpa understood intuitively that the Western work of growing up, which for him meant psychological work, and the Eastern work of waking up were two distinct lines of development, which needed to be integrated. In this tense, Chögyam Trungpa is an important forerunner of World Spirituality. Thanks to Sally Kempton for referring us to John's work. John, however, uses the term "growing up" to refer to healthy psychological growth and resolution of psychological issues within a given level of consciousness, while in the context of world spirituality we are using the term to refer to growing up to higher levels of consciousness. This recasting of these core terms was suggested by Ken Wilber who has consistently used waking up and growing up to refer to state and stage development respectively. Dustin Diperna, in his new book, *The Heart of Conscious Evolution* (San Francisco: Integral Publishing House, 2011, p. 238) suggests calling shadow work "cleaning up." I prefer the term lighten up because of its dual connotation and elegance. He also suggests using the terms "showing up" and "opening up," but in a different way then I have deployed them. I have adopted the terms much like we adopted "waking up" and "growing up" from Trungpa and changed their core meaning to

reflect the new evolutionary emergent of Unique Self. Similarly, I deploy the terms open up and show up as ways of expressing the core teachings of Unique Self enlightenment. Each of these terms is taken to express a different dimension of Unique Self. If, however, you combine my Unique Self teaching and Global Spirituality understanding, in conjunction with Ken's re-deployment of Welwood's terms to refer to states and stages, and together with Dustin Diperna's first clustering of all these terms into one package—all originally sourced in Trungpa's insight—then you have the genealogy of this wonderful and pithy formulation. Together with Ken, we are just now in the process of standardizing these usages within the World Spirituality teachings that we are co-creating. We are also adding a new category which we are calling "Storying Up" which refers to the essential post-postmodern endeavor of constructing a new world view or big picture, a new universe story which creates a context of meaning.

CPSIA information can be obtained
at www.ICGtesting.com
Printed in the USA
FSOW02n1147131014
3232FS